Why I Need Him

Why I Need Him

Stacy Rhodes

Formatted and edited by
sheliawritesbooks@yahoo.com

"For in him we live and move and have our being. As some poets have said, 'We are his offspring" (Acts 17:28 NIV).

"And my God will meet all your needs according to the riches of his glory in Christ Jesus" (Philippians 4:19 NIV).

This book is made possible by the grace of God and from many trials and life issues that draw me to Him. I would not change a thing I have been through in my life other than I wish I had given my life to God a little earlier. God has given me wisdom that I am honored to share with others.

Father, I thank you. Without you I would be drowning in excuses and not being who you called me to be. Thank you for giving me courage and for helping me push past my fears and issues in life so I could learn and be able to stand on Your Word.

Father, may this book reach the people you want it to reach and give them understanding of the words I have written. Thank you, God, for giving me these inspirational thoughts, prayers, and resources.

Table of Points

Dedication
Acknowledgements
Introduction
7 Things To Do Before Reading This Book

Dedication

To my children Anthony McClain, Marie Johnson, Gregory Rhodes Jr., Emmilia Rhodes, and Kenyetta Swift. To my beautiful grandchildren Louis Green, Emmanuel Lyles, Christian Childs, Jordan Childs, Rhianna Johnson, Payton Jade McClain, Noelle Swift, my great grandson Cartier, and great granddaughter Dream Green. Lance and D'zyre Smith and to Tae'lor. Lastly, to all who need this book—I love you all.

Acknowledgements

I thank God for giving me wisdom and strength over the years. I thank Him for maturity and for His perfect Word. I am nothing without Him and can do nothing in my own strength. But I can do all things through Him.

Thank you to my beautiful children and grandchildren. You help me stay at the feet of God.

In remembrance of my sister Jean Turner, my niece Felicia Livingston, and my brother Terrance McClain. Thank you to my mentor Audrey Johnson who went home to be with the Lord September 2021. Thank you to my brother James McClain and my sister Denise McClain who I lost before I became an adult. They always believed in me and inspired me.

To all of my family who kept me in prayer and helped me in ministry. To my sister and brothers Patricia, Kevin, and Tyrone McClain. To my nieces and nephews, thanks for putting up with me.

To everyone who prayed for me and helped me in my walk with God, thank you. Thank you Pastor Sam Moore and Lashawn Moore, my covering. Thank you for your support and desire to see God's people blessed and living their dreams.

To my church family, Conquerors Church, you guys are simply amazing. New Covenant of Peace, you will always be my family. Thank you for loving me.

A special thank you to Bishop Anthony Russell and Valerie Russell; Pastor Rueben and Darnella Edwards; Apostle Kevin Binion who sowed the Word of God and praise and worship in my life. Thank you for correcting me, crying with me, walking with me, instructing me and blessing me. You are sent from the Lord.

To Pastor Denise McCray and Faithful Priest Ministries, Jordan Missionary Baptist Church, Bishop Leonard and Lady Denise McCray, Montoya Foreman, and Annette Carter for being by my side and putting up with me at Women with Wisdom Ministry.

To my birth mom, Emily Ann McClain. In your remembrance, you were the best mom ever. I will always love you. Thank you for doing your best for me.

I thank God for Emma Hampton, my mom sent by God. Words cannot express the love I have for you. Thank you for being my sounding board and so much more.

To God be the glory for His mercy endures forever and His grace is sufficient. I love you, Lord. Thank you for loving me and believing in me when I did not love or believe in myself. Most of all, thank you, Lord, for saving me.

7 Things To Do Before Reading This Book:

1. Take a deep breath and inhale.
2. Take a moment to pray and ask God to reveal His truth.
3. Open your mind and thoughts to change.
4. Ask yourself why you are reading this book.
5. Prepare to shift the way you see and think.
6. Get ready to renew your mind and your spirit.
7. Take a moment to praise God for He is worthy of our praise.

Introduction

Many of us accept physical, verbal, spiritual, mental, emotional and sexual abuse in our lives—but why? It is time for us to take back our standards, our values, our dignity, and our virtue. Most of all it is time we take back our power to believe, trust, and love again.

The world has so many hurting people with infinite concepts, lifestyle choices, and the ability to do anything they are big enough and bad enough to do. There is so much hate, anger, selfishness, blame, fear, mistrust, unbelief and not wanting to hear the truth.

We have become a nation that lives with great technology. We can reach anyone anywhere in the world. We can get information and learn knowledge within seconds from the palms of our hands through the use of cell phones, computers, and tablets. We can email, text, and facetime anyone we choose. Yet we still face issues of uncertainty, insecurity, doubt, fear, and hopelessness combined with a faithless society.

With so many options and choices at our disposal, many of us are still unsatisfied in life, in our families, on our jobs, in our relationships, and even in the church.

I had to come to the knowledge that I needed Him after being used to doing everything on my own. I felt like if I didn't do it, it wasn't going to get done. I carried the weight of my family, my church, and my neighborhood. Sometimes I felt like the weight of the world was on my back. Thank God I came to understand I didn't have to do life alone. I had a God who loved me and a Savior named Jesus. It took time, energy, and life's problems to lead me to Him.

I hope by the time you get to the end of this book, you will not only see why I need Him but you will see and understand why *you* need Him, too. I am happy I came into the knowledge of His Word because it literally changed my life.

Why Am I So Vulnerable?

According to Dictionary.com *vulnerable* means "being susceptible to physical or emotional attack or harm of a person; in need of special care, support, or protection because of age, disability, or risk of abuse or neglect; capable of being physically or emotionally wounded; open to attack or damage."

This definition might make you feel like you are in a bad position or cause you to wonder why anyone would want to subject themselves to any of this. Unfortunately, if we want to experience love we will always be vulnerable at some point in our lives. This is why our trust should be in God alone.

Many of us are vulnerable when it comes to relationships, no matter what kind of relationship it might be. Let's start with parents and siblings. We are born into a family. We do not get to choose our parents and siblings, even if we were adopted.

We put our full trust in them as we grow up. We try to figure it out. Some of us had good parents but still have issues as we come into our independence. There are others who were not so lucky. These unlucky individuals may experience emotional, physical, or mental abuse by parents and/or siblings. This can bring devastation and cause the trust in the relationship to be destroyed. It often causes in our love walk starting early in life. This abuse, molestation, and/or ill treatment, can force a person to grow up quickly.

During the teen years, we often look and search for love in the wrong places and dysfunctional love becomes the norm. Some start using drugs, become sexually promiscuous, homeless, run away, or take on more hurt and insecurities. As they get older they continue to be involved in bad relationships. You choose friendships that mean you no good or where the other person tries to manipulate you. You pretty much take this treatment for years until it goes from bad to worse. When you become involved in a relationship, you end up choosing the wrong person, not understanding why this has become a pattern or why you can't break the cycle. This may not be your story, but you might still find yourself in this type of relationship through rebellion, being too sheltered, or from making bad choices.

God has given you the ability to love, but many of you do not understand this concept. The love you seek is in Him. He is the one who teaches you how to love. Unfortunately, some do not get to Him until late in their lives. There are others who have shown you the wrong way. I'm not speaking to those who got saved and never looked back—I am praising God for you. I am primarily talking to those who have had a little to a lot of struggle in life. Those who experienced abuse, hurt, and pain. They did not want to be vulnerable but somehow they became the victim to someone else's dysfunction and immaturity. They want to blame others, but I came to learn that some people do to us what we *allow* them to do. I am not talking about a person who was sexually violated, raped or molested.

As you grow older and you enter bad relationships, repeating the cycle of abuse, you are still being the victim. Many wonder why many women remain in abusive relationships. There are many reasons. All, or most, are dysfunctional. For instance, some say, "I know he isn't right for me, but I love him." One of my favorites is "I've been with him this long, he'll change. You watch and see." Others say the man takes care of home but yet he talks to everything that moves. There are endless reasons why women (and men too) give the excuse to stay in abusive relationships.

Many couples try to live like they are married. They shack up and get the benefits of marriage without having a real commitment. If you are not married, you are single. If there is no commitment to the person, stop living like you are married. Like the old timer says. "Why buy the cow when you can get the milk for free?"

Ladies (and gentlemen) you should take responsibility for the part you played in the relationship. Most of the time the person you are in the relationship with doesn't know how to love properly either.

Many people in relationships may not always have bad intent. They may have learned through mistreatment and/or abuse how to only love dysfunctional. There are some people who are on assignment to hinder you from what God has for you. That is why we need God to show us the truth even when it hurts.

Why am I so vulnerable? Perhaps it is because of dysfunction. Some of you are trying to fill a void within yourself which makes you open to foolishness. It can cause you to justify mess or give excuses that seem right. Vulnerability comes from the heart and head so be aware of your weaknesses. God has given us the ability to know love but sometimes people trample us and misuse our love. Some

> The New King James Bible instructs us in Proverbs 4:23 to "Keep your heart with all diligence, for out of it springs the issues of life."

show us true love with balance, but we are unable to receive it because our dysfunctional love makes us think it is out of order. But as I read and understand the Bible, it shows me the need for love which makes us vulnerable to wanting to be loved. It is a void in us that longs to be loved.

You may have heard the phrase, "I'm unlucky in love." What this person means is they have had a bad experience. Perhaps, you have heard someone say they aren't sure if they are capable of love? That's a person who is afraid to commit and probably also experienced bad relationships. The saying I like most is the one that says, "I wouldn't find love if I tripped over it." Meaning again, they have probably had unpleasant experiences when it comes to love. All this does is show the need for love. Even when people don't find love it is a place in them that knows it exists.

I believe abuse and dysfunctional relationships show a lack of being loved, being hurt, or being vulnerable. Do not think you are foolish for believing in the thought of love and being loved. Love is who God is and what He wants us to do. "Above all, love each other deeply, because love covers over a multitude of sins" (1 Peter 4:8 NIV).

Psalm 118:8 KJV states, "It is better to trust in the Lord than to put confidence in man." Jeremiah 17:5-9 KJV says, "Thus saith the Lord; cursed be the man that trusteth in man, and maketh flesh his arm, and whose heart departeth from the LORD. For he shall be like the heat in the desert, and shall not see when good cometh; but shall inhabit the parched places in the wilderness, in a salt land and not inhabited. Blessed is the man that trusteth in the Lord, and whose hope the Lord is. For he shall be as a tree planted by the waters, and that spreadeth out her roots by the river, and shall not see when heat cometh, but her leaf shall be green; and shall not be careful in the year of drought, neither shall cease from yielding fruit. The heart is deceitful above all things, and desperately wicked: who can know it?"

We cannot always be led by our hearts. Sometimes we must use wisdom and seek counseling in these life changing situations. Allow the peace of God to rule you. If we think back over our lives, we may say stuff like something told me not to do that or to leave them alone. Saved and unsaved, we get signs and flags or someone else said it and we did not want to listen. God speaks in many ways. Do not ignore the things that are placed before you. Look into your life. Let Him reign in your thoughts. Do not allow relationship choices make you feel like you need to keep being hurt. Do not remain in these types of relationships. Instead, break free and stay free with the help of making better choices, gaining understanding, and adhering to the Word of God.

Proverbs 11:14 KJV tells us, "Where there is no counsel, the people fall; but in the multitude of counselors there is safety."

Personally, in my discovery of feeling vulnerable and not wanting to trust or love again, I learned it is okay to trust and love again without feeling vulnerable, but it is only through God's Word, and His grace and mercy that I obtained it.

You need God to lead and guide you into all truth. You need Him to heal you so you can be made whole in Him. Without Him you will be stuck in an unfulfilled place or compromising relationship.

When you are in a place of being vulnerable, I believe it can be an opportunity for God to show up in your life. However, you must call on Him. Sometimes you may have to seek wise counsel. The enemy wants you to do it alone so he can have his way with us, but God never meant for us to do everything alone. We need Him for He is a present help in times of trouble.

Let us pray:

Father, thank you that I will be lead of You and Your Word. Do not let me be deceived and misused. In my state of vulnerability let me trust in You and stand on Your Word, and Your Word alone. Do not let my emotions and feelings lead me astray. Father, help me to love again, to trust again. Help me enter into healthy relationships. Allow the Holy Spirit to lead and guide me into all truth. Remove guilt and shame from my past mistakes and let me trust in You. Help me not to lean to my own understanding but to acknowledge You in all my ways, that you may direct my path. Build me up, God. Remove all doubt, fear, and hopelessness. Father, keep me covered. Help me find value in myself. Do not allow me to become caught up in my feelings or harbor bitterness, anger, and unforgiveness in my heart. Come in, Father, and create a clean heart in me. Renew a right spirit within in me. Let me live with joy. Let me love again. In Jesus' name. Amen.

Below write down areas where you are the most vulnerable. Pray and ask God to close those doors so you can experience healthy relationships Add your personal prayer or petition and watch God move on your behalf.

_____
_____
_____
_____
_____
_____

Why Am I So Needy?

I have seen relationships where a person in the relationship has a need to be loved at any cost. It's most often because they figure it is better than nothing. They remain in abusive relationships so they can say they have someone in their life. When they were working and supplying for the home their other half was playing the video game, smoking, drinking, not caring after the kids or home.

So much of this, plus a ton more abuse, went on in my childhood through my adulthood. I always wondered what happened to my siblings. I mean, we came from the same Mom. I learned they had so much hurt, anger, and disappointment that they went from being abused to being abusers. They used drugs and alcohol to ease the pain.

The Bible says, "A double-minded person is unstable in all his ways" (James 1:8 KJV). Some of you fell into how a person looked. They may have been good looking to you and you thought you had to have them in your life. That is, until they started manipulating you in the relationship. Someone you befriended or even family members you became close with might take advantage or your kindness as well.

You ask yourself why I am so needy. You're needy because you are searching to find when you became this person you've become. You ask yourself when the need to be loved took over your life.

Love is a gift from God, but as you start living life right it can get distorted because of others and because of not doing what the first commandment instructs. As you love God your love for others should line up according to His word. It is God who commands us to love.

Mark 12:30-31 NIV says, "Love the Lord your God with all your heart and with all your soul and with all your mind and with all your strength. The second is this: 'Love your neighbor as yourself.' There is no commandment greater than these."

If you're usually a kind person it is only natural that you will want to help others. You want to have friends, love your family, and be kind to others. It becomes dysfunctional when you seek this even if it causes or brings destruction, pain, turmoil or bitterness into your life. It is dysfunctional when you feel a need to stay with that person even when you know the person means you no good. That's often because your love for them has grown deeper than the love you have for yourself. If you are saved and the love you have for someone else is deeper than your love for God, that relationship is dysfunctional. It can cause confusion in many ways.

I think about my life and the times I have let others mess over me. It was often due to the choices that were focused on my love for family. I think it was because my mom said for me to always look out for family. I took what she said to heart, and it cost me a lot in my life. I remained loyal in relationships when they were all over the place. When it came to friends it seemed like I was the one that stayed loyal and gave my everything to the friendship. I learned much later in life that it was often my *yes* that allowed others to mistreat and misuse me. I didn't see the spirit of neediness back then. I always thought I was strong and independent, which I was at times, but I also see myself in a lot of the places that I talk about in this book.

I'm not judging anyone, but I do want to shine a light on hidden things in your life you need to overcome if you want to get where you need to be.

The Old Testament Book of Amos 3:3 says, "How can two walk together unless they are agreed?"

It's funny, but I was walking in agreement with the enemy and didn't even know Amos 3:3! That's what the enemy does. The moment I decided no more, the change came because then I was no longer in agreement with the need to hold on to those things that were destroying and ruining my life.

You probably heard the saying, "If you don't stand for something you'll fall for anything." This is a true statement. Please wake up. See this needy spirit for what it is in your life. We all have a place and need to be loved and to give love, but first we should learn whether it is a healthy or dysfunctional relationship. Sometimes it may not be people who we fill voids in our lives with; many of us fill voids by consuming or using material things. We say we *need* or *must have* certain material things and it becomes dysfunctional because we tend to over buy or spend. Sometimes you may get in debt or remain in bad relationships, but something keeps holding you there when you want it to just leave.

The needy spirit is mostly out of order because the Bible says, "For thou shalt worship no other god: for the Lord, whose name is Jealous, is a jealous God" (Exodus 34:14 KJV). When you put people and things before God it is not good.

Love is a gift that comes from God. It can become distorted and sometimes out of balance, but God gives us new grace and mercy daily. Every day we have another opportunity to become who God has called us to be. I urge you to put away the needy spirit that wants to keep you in unforgiveness, anger, bitterness and offense. Forgive others and forgive yourself, so you can be made whole again.

John 10:10 says, "The thief comes only to steal and kill and destroy; I have come that they may have life, and have it to the full" (NIV). I asked God about this scripture because I did not quite understand it. If we are killed then how can we be destroyed? He comes to steal first. The enemy wants to steal your joy, peace, innocence, your ability to love, trust, and believe. Then he kills your spirit, your ability to see and hear Him. Next, he destroys your soul because you walked according to the flesh. This changed my life when I saw and understood the scripture this way.

Sometimes we remain in relationships because they seem harmless, but these kinds of relationships can often stunt your growth with God. You might find yourself at a standstill and feel content when God has so much more. The need to stay will have you staying in a dead-end relationship. You might think you won't find anyone better, but you have been in the relationship 5-10 years, and the person won't even marry you! You are living in sin, living like you're married, dating like you're married, but you haven't even been given a good friendship ring. Remember, you are single unless you are married.

Before I learned the Word, I was in an unhappy, long-term relationship. Don't get it twisted, he was very good to me, but there was a void. Even with all the provisions and love, I wanted more. I started learning the Word and wanted my walk to line up with my life. It was hard. I had to pray my way out of it but through God's grace, mercy and a lot of prayer I made it. God set me free and now I am satisfied with my life. God can do the same for you. I am not judging anyone, but I am trying to expose the enemy. When God has a plan, it will always come to fullness.

Have you ever thought you should be doing more or be a little farther in your life, but then we say everything is good. What if God is pushing you toward greatness. If you are blessed and no one else is benefitting from it then you have not reached the place God is calling you. God wants us blessed. He sees more than we see in ourselves. He wants us to reach our full potential.

1 Thessalonians 5:23 says, "Now may the God of peace Himself sanctify you completely; and may your whole spirit, soul, and body be preserved blameless at the coming of our Lord Jesus Christ" (NKJV).

Being needy can limit you from reaching your destiny because people will become a crutch. That is not of God. God tells us to put our trust in Him. Your wholeness should be in God. Our mates should enhance us, not complete us. That's a God job.

Once I let go, things changed. I found wholeness in Christ. I thank God for opening my eyes to greater and not staying stuck in compromise. Once I got away from the thought of needing them, I could see more clearly. I saw my mistakes in my relationships. I was giving others power over me that did not belong to them in the first place. So, if your life has a place to depend on others, it's okay. Make sure it is not out of order or unbalanced. You and God should always have the most stock in your life, in your relationships, in your marriages, in your families, on your job, and every area of your life. I am sharing truth and knowledge so you can have victory in your life.

So, forgive, grow, and move on into victory. Start your walk into healing and purpose. Sometimes the people who hurt you are those who are near and dear to your heart (i.e. parents, children, siblings, friends, spouses, church leaders, bosses, business partners, girlfriend, boyfriend, etc.). Even our government is failing us. God says, "It is better to trust in the Lord than to put confidence in man" (Psalms 118:8 KJV).

Some people believe it is God who has let them down. If the truth be told, we cannot always blame God, but He can take it. We who are strong ought to bear the infirmities of the weak. Our emotions are always looking to find answers or find blame. We often wonder why there is so much evil, pain, confusion. It's because every man has a choice to choose right or wrong.

Poor choices can change, ruin, or end your life. We all need something or someone to help bring balance into our lives. Have you ever had an experience where you are thinking of speeding through a traffic light or stop sign and something tells you not to? I have and it saved my life. Understand that your choices can help change your destiny.

Being too needy is a true sign that you're on the brink of being hurt or used by those who are out for selfish gain. Sometimes our need to blame others needs a little balance. Sometimes the spirit that makes us need to be loved and needed can become a false source of comfort and a false sense of love. If I need you more than I love you, it is out of balance so be aware of your need for others. Do not confuse needing with loving.

Let us pray:

Father, thank you for bringing balance to our lives. Thank you for keeping us safe from being prey to those who like to manipulate and are out for selfish gains. Do not let us be so needy that we cannot see ourselves being out of order. If we have been hurt, bring healing. Help us learn how to forgive those who misused us. Bring balance to our decision-making. Help us break free from every situation keeping us bound. Bring back hope and trust so that we can live again. Father, speak life in those areas where our emotions and trust have died inside. Give us clarity. Help us make better decisions. Help us fill the void of needing wrong things and instead help us to seek you for balance and fulfilment. We thank you. We give you praise for changing us. Thank you for helping us to be strong and finding peace from the cares of the world. Help us know that it is okay to need others but let us keep balance. Father, we thank you that the healing process shall begin. In Jesus' name. Amen.

Ask God to fill the voids in your life. Write down these voids so you can know when He has filled them:

_____

_____

_____

_____

_____

_____

_____

_____

_____

_____

_____

_____

_____

_____

_____

_____

Why Am I So Insecure?

Many things can bring harm to our lives when we are insecure. I have addressed eight of them.

1. Fear of judgment

Fear is often described as *false evidence appearing real.* When you are insecure, you often live in fear about what others think and you think the worst.

When you think the worst and believe the worst you can cause harm and unneeded stress into your life. You cannot see clearly when you are fearful. It is a horrible way to live. I know, because I have lived in fear before. I talk more about this in my other book "Free to Be Me."

With all the confusion and mess going on in the world today, people seem unable to move and the phobia is only getting stronger and crazier. However, the Word of God says in 2 Timothy 1:7 KJV, "For God hath not given us the spirit of fear; but of power, and of love, and of a sound mind."

When I first started going to Bible study we had to read scriptures out loud. I would tell everyone I was shy and not ready yet. I didn't finish high school so I wouldn't read aloud for a while. Fear had me believing I wouldn't be able to pronounce all the words, and that others were going to think I was dumb and that I couldn't read. As I got more into the Word, I grew stronger in my walk and my courage grew stronger.

I went back to school and earned my G.E.D. I made excellent grades and soon I began loving to read. I realized it was the enemy that was trying to hold me back from where I was headed. If I would have listened, I might still be stuck in that area.

God wants you to step out of fear. Do not worry about being judged. People persecuted Jesus and you can never please everyone. Be who you are. Let God use you for His glory. He loves you. "Therefore let us stop passing judgment on one another. Instead, make up your mind not to put any stumbling block or obstacle in the way of a brother or sister" (Romans 14:13 NIV).

2. You Avoid Meeting and Trusting People

Some of you do not like interacting with other people because you fear they might not like you. You see your own flaws. You know the insecurities that people don't see. You do not want to let your insecurities leak out so you distance yourself. You might believe others will not think you're interesting or educated enough so you remain quiet. This used to describe me, until I learned the enemy wanted me quiet because he knew I had so much locked up in me that could help others be set free. I did not want to socialize with others in fear of being judged.

The enemy wants you to keep to yourself. He does not want you or me to help others. When I think back on my life and see the difference God has made and how He now uses me to set others free from being insecure, it is a shock.

God wants to use you to set others free, too. He has so much in store for you. Psalm 56:3-4 NIV says, "When I am afraid, I put my trust in you. In God, whose word I praise—in God I trust and am not afraid. What can mere mortals do to me?"

3. Not Good Enough

I can give a sermon on this one—being bound, feeling not good enough, being molested, raped, in an abusive marriage, making bad choices, being a single mom, and with just a G.E.D. Trust me, I thought I had nothing to offer anyone. I believed I was a good mom and a loyal person but that was it. I believed nobody wanted to hear what I had to say.

Insecurity can leave you feeling this way, but for me, when I began to study the Word of God, my walk with Him grew stronger. At the same time I learned my true value. I learned that I am more than a conqueror through him that loves me (Romans 8:37 NIV).

I want you to understand that you also have something to offer others. There are people who want and need to hear what you have to say. God wants you to share your testimony. Remember, no one can tell your story better than you. Revelations 12:11 NIV says, "They triumphed over him by the blood of the Lamb and by The Word of their testimony; they did not love their lives so much as to shrink from death."

4. Being Untrue To Yourself

Many of you are not comfortable with who you are, so you try to fit in and adapt to your social situations. You might even try to become like someone else.

I remember times I would go out with my friends and my brothers. Sometimes people would ask me why I was hanging around with them at a particular place because they said it didn't fit me. I didn't understand what they were talking about because, like them, I grew up with the very people I was hanging around with. Other people would say there was something different about me.

Feeling insecure about yourself can make you think there's something bad about you when that's not true. God says otherwise. God says, we are uniquely made so that means different. He made us the way we are for His purpose and His plan. Psalm 139:14 NIV says, "I praise you because I am fearfully and wonderfully made…"

5. Living In Denial

When you are insecure, you usually do not want to see or hear facts. You often bypass them and rather believe the worst. This can cause you to stay in a bad situation.

When I was in my abusive marriage I knew when the abuse was coming. It would be after my husband had been out all night drinking and partying. When it was time for the rent and bills to be paid, he wouldn't have it. I saw it coming ahead of time and mentally prepared myself.

The facts of what was happening told me to get out and live in peace, but my insecurity told me my kids would grow up without a father. Turns out they *did* grow up without a father but they turned out well.

God does not want us leaning to our own understanding. He knows the thoughts He thinks of us. They are better than our thoughts for sure. Do not allow the enemy to play with your mind. Jeremiah 29:11 NIV says, "For I know the plans I have for you," declares the LORD, "plans to prosper you and not to harm you, plans to give you hope and a future."

I encourage you to allow God to help you see truth in your life. He does not want you to be deceived. God sees us differently than we see ourselves. If only you could see yourself through His eyes.

2 Corinthians 2:11 NIV warns, "…in order that Satan might not outwit us. For we are not unaware of his schemes."

Some of the devices Satan uses are lying, reasoning, doubt, instability, fear, manipulation, and deception. He presents himself as a smooth talker. Satan never stops trying to get you to go against God's Word by pulling it out of context. The good news is no matter how many devices Satan has or uses, God is greater than them all.

6. You Are Doomed To Fail

I remained in an abusive marriage far too long because my feelings of insecurity made me believe it was better to have both parents in the household rather than one. I thought my children would have a better life with two parents because the world says people who grow up with both parents have a better success rate. I know some amazing single mothers whose children turned out well, mine included. I am so glad that God defeated that stage in my life.

Many believe you are doomed if you fail to try, but His Word says in Psalm 68:5-6 NLT says, "Father to the fatherless, defender of widows—this is God, whose dwelling is holy. God places the love in families; he sets the prisoners free and gives them joy. But he makes the rebellious live in a sun-scorched land."

7. When You Are Insecure, You Don't Trust Others

Not trusting others can cause you to miss out on good and godly relationships, but because you experienced a bad relationship it makes it hard for you to trust again. It may even be hard to trust God when you first come into the knowledge of Him because of the bad things that have happened in your life or around you.

With this particular point, I want to talk about my relationship with God. At first, it was a battle for me to trust God in my walk because of what others had done to me. It was a learning experience in which I had to come into the knowledge, but more importantly, a relationship with Him to be able to trust Him. He is so amazing. It took me from baby steps to walking in His trust and not mine. Proverbs 3:5 NIV says, "Trust in the Lord with all your heart; do not depend on your own understanding."

It is like building a relationship; you must get in God's presence, learn His voice and His word. The more you draw closer to Him, the more you will be able to see God leading and guiding you into truth. In that, deliverance can take place and you can start trusting again.

8. Looking For The Worst

Many people go around looking for and expecting the worst. For instance, you worry about what will happen if you get into another relationship. Will it work? What if you start a business and it fails or no one comes to an event you planned. What if you write a book and no one buys it? You entertain one worry after another, expecting the worst.

I'm telling you to go forth and trust God to help you along the way. There will always be what ifs and bouts with fear but you can choose not to be part of it with God's strength, and not your own. Place your trust in Him. I can tell you for sure that He will show up for you.

Genesis 28:15 NIV says, "I am with you and will watch over you wherever you go, and I will bring you back to this land. I will not leave you until I have done what I have promised you." This particular passage of scripture reassures us we are not alone. We have an advocate working on our behalf at all times.

When the enemy tries to mess with your mind you can fight back with the Word. When you are insecure you are not rooted in the reality of what God can do, will do, and is able to do in your life.

Defeat negative thoughts, negative ideas, negative people and even self-negativity. Go after and seek the promises God has for you instead.

Sometimes you can be your own worst enemy. Life may have beaten you down. You may feel as if life has not been the best, but remember you have an opportunity to change and do better through the Word of God.

"Finally, brothers and sisters, whatever is true, whatever is noble, whatever is right, whatever is pure, whatever is lovely, whatever is admirable—if anything is excellent or praiseworthy—think about such things" (Philippians 4:8 NIV).

"....casting down imaginations, and every high thing that exalteth itself against the knowledge of God, and bringing into captivity every thought to the obedience of Christ" (2 Corinthians 10:5-6 KJV).

Insecurity can cause you to miss what God has planned for you. Insecurity can cause you to draw away and hold back what is inside of you. It can make you fearful of living life. It can cause you not to trust, hope, or want to try love again.

I am so happy God allowed me to become free so I can help others and have a better life for myself and my family.

God wants you to be free. He knows there is something in you that someone needs to hear. There is so much love in you to share and so much knowledge in you that someone needs to hear. Most of all, there is so much more you need to experience and share. You are more than a conqueror. You can

have victory over your insecurities. You may not see it but it is there. I know this because I have written this book when my insecurities tried to convince me that no one would listen. If I would have listened to my insecurity, I would be stuck in my thoughts. But God! "No, in all these things we are more than conquerors through him who loved us" (Romans 8:37 NIV).
Let us pray:

Father, thank you that you hear my prayers and will answer. Remove all areas where I am insecure. Bring me to the knowledge of who you say I am and what I say I can do. Let me trust again, love again, and be comfortable in being myself and not who others are trying to make me to be. Father, I have been bound for so long. I need you to set me free.

Thank you for sending the Word and I will study to show myself approved. As I do, it will strengthen and encourage me and bring me to the person you have called me to be. I will not be quiet. I will not blend in. I will not go against Your Word and become my own worst enemy. My thoughts will line up with Your Word as I cast down every imagination that exalts itself against the knowledge of God and lets me bring into captivity every thought to the obedience of Christ.

Father, set me free of all my phobias, fears, and the cares of what others think. You have not given me the spirit of fear so give me wisdom and understanding of how to defeat the negative doom and gloom spirit that dwells in me. Bring me to a place of freedom. Expose the hand of the enemy and deliver me. I ask you to help me become secure in YOU, Father.

Below, write down your insecurities so you can see when God brings you out.

_____
_____
_____
_____
_____
_____
_____
_____

Stacy Rhodes

Why Am I So Comfortable?

Have you ever thought about why you are comfortable in messy situations that hurt you or that you know are no good for you? Have you ever wondered why you tolerate these types of relationships? I believe it comes from a place of being comfortable to the point where it feels like you don't have another choice, or you don't want to deal with it. You may want to keep the peace even though it caused or causes you pain. You know the relationship has hit its peak or you know you are in a dead-end job or partnership; you know the person means you no good but you stay because you have become settled and comfortable.

I think about times in my life when I let people run over me. It was not because I was weak but because of the love I had for them. Sometimes people can be selfish and inconsiderate. They may not always try to hurt you. Sometimes they believe it's simply who they are and they are doing what was done to them. It may also be a spirit of manipulation.

Hurt people hurt people is a true statement, even in ministry. Many times you tolerate stuff until it becomes the norm when it shouldn't. You lose respect and dignity, your self-esteem, and become mad, bitter, or take it out on others.

The tolerance we have as a people is crazy. You may be able to withstand a lot but that doesn't make it good. Sometimes your ability to love can be scary and take you places you can't come back from. I have been in that place.

My ex-husband tried to take my life. He was about to shoot me in the head, but God intervened and the clip fell out. His pride and anger told him if he couldn't have me no one could. I look back on it all and think how I made it through. It was God.

It seems strange how the things I tried to save my children from are some of the same problems they have encountered as adults. They fight the same problems and their children face some of the same problems. I guess I never looked at how much of a role genetics plays in a person's life other than looks.

> 1Peter1:23 KJV says, "being born again, not of corruptible seed, but of incorruptible, by the Word of God, which liveth and abideth forever."

Five things you can pass down from DNA are genetics, height, skin color, eye color, and build. Our health can be significantly influenced but the specific genetic code influences our biology. Risks of obesity, high blood pressure, and allergies are notable health traits often passed down through DNA. Think about being born again and you take on the trait of Jesus Christ. God gives us promises in His Word about life. If you are in Christ, His promise is "With long life, will I satisfy him, shew him my salvation" (Psalm 91:16 KJV).

Intelligence is a tricky trait to pinpoint. The Holy Spirit gives us God's wisdom. It is just as powerful as being intelligent. The world wants us to focus on so much other than God, but if you are saved, you should live by the Word. "For the Lord giveth wisdom: out of his mouth cometh knowledge and understanding" (Proverb 2:6 KJV).

Our extraversion, psychological interests, openness to new experiences, and conscientiousness are also linked to our DNA. Personality and emotionalism are genetic effects which can influence our social lives. How you response to stress and your feelings are biologically correlated. Imagine if we used the Word as He did. Psalm 119:105 KJV tells us, "Your word is a lamp for my feet, a light on my path."

Genetics can influence our talents and abilities. We can mold our behavior to change our genetics. Genes do not dictate our existence. They can be turned on and off by experience and environment, but the Word of God talks about us having gifts and talents He has given us.

We need God to remove generational curses and renew our minds to the way He says we should be thinking and receiving. Romans 12:2 KJV instructs "Do not be conformed to the pattern of this world, but be transformed by the renewing of your mind. Then you will be able to test and approve what God's will is – his good, pleasing perfect will."

So yes, we get comfortable for many reasons but do not stay there because God has so much more for you. Here some scriptures to encourage you: "...Greater is he that is in you than he that in this world" (1 John 4:4 KJV).

I believe life is better when you give your life to Christ. For me, it was the best decision I ever made. This is what the Word says happens when you give your life to Christ. "If you confess with your mouth Jesus is Lord and believe in your heart that God raised him from the dead, you will be saved, for it is with the heart that you believe and are justified, and it is with your mouth you confess and are saved ... for everyone who calls on the name of the lord will be saved" (Romans 10:9-10, 13 KJV).

"According as he hath chosen us in him before the foundation of the world, that we should be holy and without blame before him in love: Having predestinated us unto the adoption of children by Jesus Christ to himself, according to the good pleasure of his will" (Ephesians 1:4-5).

"Therefore, if any man be in Christ, he is a new creature: old things have passed away. Behold, all things are become new" (2 Corinthians 5:17 KJV).

Some traits we inherit after we become believers:

"That you be not slothful but followers of those who through faith and patience inherit the promises" (Hebrews 6:12 KJV)

"But now hath he obtained a more excellent ministry, by how much also he is the mediator of a better covenant, which was established upon better promises" (Hebrews 8:6 KJV).

"For all the promises of God in him are yea, and in him Amen, unto the glory of God by us" (2 Corinthians 1:20 KJV).

So, being comfortable is not necessarily a bad thing, but sometimes better is waiting on the other side. Being comfortable is more like settling. You should want God's best. You should want to live in peace. I love my natural family but

I love my spiritual family too. I said this to say my natural family's love does not change because of their actions. I deal with them differently. I get away from the drama, issues, and dysfunction because the Word enlightens and helps me see that the way I was living was incorrect. With my spiritual family, I found God's Word is true. I love and thank God for them as well.

"But he answered and said unto him that told him, Who is my mother? and who are my brethren? And he stretched forth his hand toward his disciples, and said, Behold my mother and my brethren! For whosoever shall do the will of my Father which is in heaven, the same is my brother, and sister, and mother" (Matthew 12:48-50).

Let us pray:

Father, teach us how to override any genetic traits we receive from our parents that are not good for us, and give us the strength to do so. Remind us of the promises that come when we are born again so we do not have to remain in situations that cause us pain. Do not let us stay in a system designed for us to fail and stay stagnate.

Father, help us to receive our spiritual family as well as our natural family. Help us to love them with your love. Show us how to recognize any dysfunction in our relationships. Bring balance to every area of our lives, including ministry.

Father, help us to remove ourselves and our children away from the hand of the enemy. Let our women and men not live according to their enticement or flesh, but let us see you have so much more for our lives, marriages, families, and ministries. Let us shine so men can see you and give You the glory. Remove us out of places where we should not be. Amen.

Below, please list places, situations, and things you want God to deliver you from.

_____

_____

_____

Why Am I the Only One In Love?

Have you ever been head over hills in love, giving all you had to make sure your significant other was happy, but they are not committed to you or the relationship? Most of us have seen all kinds of relationships. When those relationships are unhealthy, you may try to tell them they are being misused and taking advantage of.

I have witnessed many unhealthy relationships in my lifetime. I have witnessed the person ending up alone and devastated. Sometimes I think it is because we have made these people like an idol in our lives. God does not like this. He does not want us to put anything or anyone before Him.

These unhealthy relationships may also come from not receiving wisdom from others, being disobedient, not seeking wise counsel, and allowing our flesh to run our emotions, feelings, and ability to reason.

Some people have had thoughts of committing suicide because of these unhealthy type of relationships. Others have succeeded in taking their own lives. These thoughts and actions are demonic. The enemy wants you to believe that there is no one else for you. If the troubled person refuses counseling and does not have a relationship with God, it will be hard to help them.

The greatest love story ever told for me was when Jesus died on the cross so we can have life and have it more abundantly. That is what I call love. God truly does love us. He gave His only begotten son. You can be free from all forms of bondage.

It is okay to *want* to be in love and to be loved, but to stay in love with someone who is causing you hurt is not part of God's purpose. James 1:17 NIV says "Every good and perfect gift is from above, coming down from the father of the heavenly lights, who does not change like shifting shadows."

So, the person that is taking advantage of you may not be from God. That person may not be who God has for you. If you're in this kind of relationship you can be free. Believe that God has someone who will love you, but first you must let go of the person who doesn't love you. Being in love by yourself never fulfills you. You are left filling empty. I hope you are able to get free from the thought of being in love and causing self -harm. It can be hard to watch those we love get hurt in these unhealthy relationships. I pray that God will break the bondage and set you and anyone free from these types of relationships. I pray that you will live, laugh, love, and be loved again.

I've seen and experienced many things in my life. I learned and gleamed from these experiences. This is why I am sharing wisdom and truth in this day and hour.

Let us pray:

Father, set us free from the spirit of being in love with the idea of being in love. Help us break free from the destructive spirit of being misused and abused. When something or someone is harmful and out of order with Your Word, help us to recognize this and then set us free from it. Let us lay down the idol of love and worshipping a person or anything more than we worship you. Help us to break free from being in love with someone who does not love us and only wants to mistreat us. Let us stop hurting our family and friends with these selfish acts.

Deliver us from our own lust and wrongful thinking. Lord, we need to fill this void with YOU so we can be healed and made whole. Time is short; do not let us waste anymore love or any more time being in love by ourselves. Show us how to break this toxic mindset and begin the healing process. In Jesus' name. Amen.

Pray and ask God to help you to love correctly. Write down every bad relationship, forgive the person (including yourself), and move on.

_____

_____

_____

_____

_____

_____

_____

_____

_____

_____

_____

_____

_____

_____

_____

_____

_____

_____

_____

_____

_____

_____

_____

_____

_____

_____

_____

_____

_____

_____

_____

_____

_____

_____

_____

Why Am I Jealous and Bitter?

Jealousy is described, depending on different dictionaries, as *being unhappy or angry because of what someone else has, or the belief that someone you love likes or is liked by someone else.* Jealousy can stem from low self-esteem, poor self-image, and unrealistic expectations about relationships. The emotion of jealousy is a form of shame. Jealousy can breed suspicion, mistrust, or a fear of being betrayed. It can make us possessive of people. It can bring about feelings of insecurity, fear, resentment, inadequacy, helplessness, and disgust. We normally have it against a rival, or a person enjoying success.

Jealousy can destroy relationships and eat away at you inside and out. Jealousy is something that is in your thoughts. God says in 2 Corinthians 10:5, "Casting down imaginations, and every high thing that exalteth itself against the knowledge of God, and bringing into captivity every thought to the obedience of Christ." Bad thoughts and negative thoughts will always lead you wrong. I believe that negative thoughts are sent to derail you and keep you from living peaceful and productive lives.

You should not be jealous of others or want what they have. I believe many people think others have better lives than them. Sometimes the person's life you're yearning to have may want someone else's life. The grass may look greener on the other side but that doesn't make it true. Looks can be deceiving. There is always someone less fortunate and with more problems than you. Even those with money have problems. Jealousy makes you feel like a victim but we are to think good thoughts.

The Bible tells us in Philippians 4:8 KJV, "Finally, brethren, whatsoever things are true, whatsoever things are honest, whatsoever things are pure, whatsoever things are lovely, whatsoever things are good report, if there is virtue, and if there be any praise, think on these things"

This is why jealousy should be overcome. Nothing good comes out of jealousy. It pushes others away and leaves hurt feelings. It brings forth bitterness after dwelling on it. I am not judging or condemning you. I am trying to change your thought patterns. Ask God to search your heart; He knows you best.

Psalm 139:14 KJV, David says, "I will praise thee, for I am fearfully and wonderfully made, marvelous are thy works: and that my soul knoweth right well." Thank God that you are you. Do not focus on what others have. Accept and receive your uniqueness because there is only *one* you.

Take a moment to confess the sinner's prayer. "If you confess with your mouth the Lord Jesus and believe in your heart that God raised him from the dead you will be saved" Romans 10:9 NIV. Now you can obtain this promise.

So celebrate others. Celebrate their victories and successes. Do what is right in the sight of God and you will be blessed.

If jealousy goes undealt with it will turn into bitterness and then unforgiveness until it destroys or hinders you. Bitterness is deep anger that lingers. You can't or won't let go of whatever was done

Psalm 84:11KJV says, For the Lord God is a sun and shield: the Lord will give grace and glory: no good thing will he withhold from them that walk uprightly."

to you. You want to *see* the other person get what you think they deserve. Bitterness can cause you to have wicked and evil thoughts toward those who wronged you. Meditate on the following scriptures.

Leviticus 19:18 NIV says, "Do not seek revenge or bear a grudge against anyone among your people, but love your neighbor as yourself. I am the Lord."

Romans 12:19 NIV, "Do not take revenge, my dear friends, but leave room for God's wrath, for it is written: "It is mine to avenge; I will repay," says the Lord."

1 John 4:20 NIV, "Whoever claims to love God yet hates a brother or sister is a liar. For whoever does not love their brother and sister, whom they have seen, cannot love God, whom they have not seen.

1 John 2:9 NIV, "Anyone who claims to be in the light but hates a brother or sister is still in the darkness."

Leviticus 19:17 ESV, "You shall not hate your brother (sister) in your heart, but you shall reason frankly with your neighbor, lest you incur sin because of them."

Jealousy and bitterness is bondage. You must get free from it if you want to live in peace and have joy in your life. Do not let the enemy have that much power over you. Forgive them and forgive yourself so you can be right with God and be free.

Let us pray:

Father, thank you that we will be set free from jealousy and bitterness. Thank you that we will forgive and carry out our destiny in you. Let us put down every weight that so easily besets us. Let us reunite with any loved ones we have fallen out with. Let us lay down our pride and selfish thoughts. Father, let us see as you see us. Let us be healed in the areas where we are weak.

Give us the words and opportunity to make things right with those still here and release to you those who have passed away. Let us forgive those who caused harm and hurt to us. We pray that you touch them as well.

Father, sometimes we can't see beyond our own hurt and pain, but you said we can be healed so start the process and we will trust you to open doors for us to apologize and give the receiver the grace to receive them. Let us build back relationships that were lost. We thank you for courage and strength to at least try and deliver us from the root of jealousy and bitterness as we get into Your Word. Deliver us from wanting justice and our own way. Instead, let us place everything in your hands. In Jesus' name. Amen.

Write down your hurt and disappointments: Pray and ask God to heal you from each hurt and give you peace.

_____

_____

_____

Why Am I So Willing To Compromise?

As human beings, we compromise for good and bad reasons. Sometimes in the midst of situations in life we lose balance and end up compromising to the wrong things at the wrong times. For instance, marriage can be amazing when it is in the right concept. But sometimes it gets out of balance when one spouse uses it in abuse and brings emotional turmoil. When you see that there is a miscommunication between the two or you, but you talk about it rather than have a huge fight, that is a good thing.

What should be done in a situation like the following? Your spouse wants the two of you to become swingers. He/She convinces you that it will be okay because he/she says the two of you have a good strong marriage and relationship. You go along with the swinging session but afterward your spouse leaves you because they found more pleasure with someone else.

The above scenario is wrong on so many levels. First, it is adultery. Second, you may be strong but you open doors for all kinds of demons and sin to enter. Third, now the bed is defiled in your marriage. You don't know what happened or how the marriage ended up here. Exodus 20:14 KJV, "Thou shall not commit adultery."

> Hebrews 13:4 KJV, "Marriage is honorable in all, and the bed undefiled: but whoremongers and adulterers God will judge."

The enemy is always looking to set us up and to destroy that which is good. Now, let's turn to our children. For example, as a parent you decide you will compromise by letting your child be *themselves*. You are going to be a friend to them first. You later discover your child or "friend" has taken twenty dollars out of your purse, but you say it's no big deal. Next, they take a candy bar from the store—again, no big deal. At age eleven they take a watch from grandma's jewelry box without correction or talking to. At 18 when they steal a car, you say you have no idea where your child got this type of behavior from because certainly you didn't teach him/her to steal. Well, no correction *is* teaching them there are no consequences for their behavior. As a parent, you should have taught them if you did not ask then it is stealing.

When he/she stole the candy bar you should have told your child to apologize and take it back. Maybe it would have saved your child from being that person doing wrong. I believe it operates the same in relationships when you compromise your integrity, values, dignity, and respect to stay in a bad relationship when you know the other person does not have your best interest at heart and is using and manipulating you.

You are compromising your children's safety by being in relationships with men and women who are abusing them mentally, physically, sexually, and it can be spiritually as well. Stop compromising when it comes down to your child's safety. Some children do not come back from it, while others it takes a lifetime to heal. It is so bad now. You have people who are raping newborns, killing your children, shaking and beating them to death.

As parents, you should be aware of who you allow to watch your kids. Not just anyone will do. God has entrusted you to watch over them. Someone told me I must be exhausted because with all I do, I always have my grandkids with me. That is true. I have them because until they are of the age where they can speak for themselves, I will be right there. I am sowing into them while I can. I'm never too tired where I would turn them over to wolves in sheep clothing—never. That is how the enemy destroys families. He divides and conquers. Families used to be strong. Oh, my God, it's like we cannot get along anymore.

Romans 8: 28 NIV: "And we know that all things work for the good of those who love him, who have been called according to his purpose."

Compromising is not worth the damage it can cause. I urge you to stop compromising. If you wait on God, He can and will work things out for your good.

I was one of those children who was molested and raped. The enemy wanted to make me quiet and live in fear but now I can write this book and help set others free. Proverbs 22:6 KJV: "Train up a child in the way he should go, and when he is old he will not depart from it." God is saying, if we raise our children in the standard of the Word they will do what is right. If we raise them up with secrets, lies, stealing, not caring, selfishness, being manipulative, with evil then they will be led by the enemy. They will keep doing wrong and will not depart from it. So, unless God and truth intervene, watch what and how you are raising your children. Do not always compromise in bad cases. Use wisdom when compromising to make sure it is productive and good. Use wisdom and good judgment.

God tells us in Psalm 119:3 NLT, "They do not compromise with evil, and they walk only in his paths."

There are so many more words of wisdom in this chapter. He says further in Psalm 15:2 KJV, "He that walketh uprightly, and worketh righteousness, and speaketh the truth in his heart."

I will close out on this note. Compromise is good in balance and with good intention, but it can be tragic on the other side. If it costs you your respect, values, dignity, honor, your children, hurt, harm, puts you in danger, in debt, takes away from you, costs you your peace, and much more then know that you are probably compromising to the wrong thing. Compromising should be fair, just, good, and peaceful if it is in the right aspect. Do not give into the spirit of compromise if it leaves you empty, frustrated, angry, unfulfilled and stagnated in life. God has so much more for you.

God wants you to live a good life without thinking you have to settle. God knows what is best for you and your family too. And remember the choices we make affect others around us. Remember, you are the apple of God's eyes. Get up, try again, and see what things can be a benefit instead of a burden. See what can bring value and not take away from you. See what can enhance you or build you up and not tear you down. You can find all these things in God's Word. You also need people around who will push you and not let you compromise in important areas of your life and major decisions.

I was working on getting my book out by a certain date for my book event when my publisher emailed me and said, "'*You need to fix this.*'" I rushed, still trying to make my deadline. She emailed me a second time and said, "'No, this is still not ready. Take another look because something is missing. If you want me to, I can fix it but I feel like you are rushing.'"

At that point, I called her because I know she will always be a real person with me, and it is not about money with her. As we shared with one another, we were both thinking the same thing. I trusted her and knew she had my best interest at heart. I thank God for our connection and her honesty. She was correct. I had so much going on in my life that it was showing through the pages. When I settled down and looked at it to restful eyes, I agreed with her. I asked myself *who is writing this book?* I hope when I send it in this time it will be ready to publish.

Yes, people pat your ego, but God makes you whole. I would rather have friends that tell me the truth rather than let me make bad choices.

Wisdom tells you to listen. Compromise tells you that you're okay. There is *healthy* and *unhealthy* compromise. That is why I need Him; so I can make the right decisions. He will bring wisdom, peace, and people in my life that will push me to be better and not compromise.

Let us pray:

Father, help us to stop compromising with the enemy and with ourselves. Let us understand that time is short and we have been bound long enough. For many of us, it has cost us relationships, our children, our values, our respect, dignity, and honor. It has cost us wasted time in our walk with You. For others, it has cost jobs, partnerships, friends, parents and siblings relationships, and some much more. Father, give us wisdom and the skill to compromise with balance.

We need your help now. So much time has been lost and so much damage done. There are some precious relationships that only you can heal and make whole again. Father, mend broken relationships. Teach us to wait on You. Hear and our prayers. Help us make healthy and not unhealthy compromises in our lives. Cover our mistakes and bad choices. Let us not live in guilt or shame but give us the strength and courage to face our past so we can have a bright future with you. Remove fear, anxiety, guilt, shame, and doubt. Help us to forgive ourselves and others. Bring peace, hope, trust, fresh starts, and new beginnings. In Jesus' name. Amen.

Ask God for balance and discernment. Write down what you want and need from Him.

Why Am I So Independent?

According to Google dictionary, the word *independent* means *to be free from outside control, not depending on another's authority*. For instance, most 18 year olds can't wait to get out of their parents' house and from under their authority. They believe to be *independent* is great, that there's nothing like being in charge of all your decisions, no one is telling you what to do, how to live, or how to spend your money. Being 18 may make you grown *legally* but that does not mean the 18-year-old is mature and independent. The majority that does well may be the ones who are mature and have learned the value of a dollar. Others have not. What I have come to learn is that once things get out of balance it becomes something we have to deal with. No matter what the meaning I believe we are always subjected to some authority.

My sisters, even after they left home and had their own homes, were still not fully independent. There was still a landlord having authority over them. Your new authority comes along in the form of your bosses and employers. Oh yes and do not forget Uncle Sam.

Therefore, my question is this—are we ever really independent? After my divorce I promised myself I would not depend on anyone. For years I was that person who would not ask for help. As a woman, I believe being hurt or becoming a single mom, I tried even harder to prove I did not need anyone. I guess God has a way to make you call on Him.

My children were my everything. When my daughter got pregnant it made me realize I needed someone. When she got pregnant it hurt me because I wanted better for my children than I had for myself. It humbled me from thinking I was super mom.

When my spiritual mom invited me to church it was like the pastor was talking to me. I kept going to church and I haven't turned from God since. He taught me that in life I will always answer to someone or something so I should use wisdom to make good choices. Being independent caused me a lot of hurt, pain, brokenness, and sorrow internally. Outwardly, I kept it together for the sake of my children and family. I needed God to find peace and to be made whole. In my independence I made many mistakes and bad choices. I thank God I found a God that knew and wanted to make me whole again. I laid down my independence and picked up Jesus, which means I am subject to a higher authority.

There were times when I was trying not to be under any authority. I was working like a slave and running like one too, trying to keep it all together. I didn't realize at the time how much it took to be a single working mom, and friend while taking care of my family. I was also trying to find my salvation, healing, deliverance, and myself. I can't say it was being independent but more like living in bondage to the enemy. I didn't have a mom to run back to or any family to run to because I took care of *them*.

Independence may sound great but if you're not ready, don't be so quick to be on your own. Wait, save your money so when you do leave you will be established and prepared to have a good and stable life.

You may have seen someone you loved fail after trying to get away from authority. They learned the hard way— through heartbreak, abuse, getting in debt, instead of using wisdom and listening to advice from those who have been through it.

Some people want their independence so they can party and hang out. Partying and hanging out drinking and getting high may have been fun for a minute until that leads to not getting up on time for work or getting sick at work. Drinking can turn into taking someone home with you after the party. A real case in point could be you end up pregnant or worst they slept with you and then they stop calling. Either way, you're broken and also pregnant. Your *independence* has cost you something because once the child is born, you are no longer independent. You have a dependent and it demands a lot of your time. See the traps set for you. Let's not even talk about sexual diseases and the backlash of being talked about. I'm saying all this to hopefully keep you focused on the task at hand.

I believe God is saying enough of letting the enemy lay traps and us leaving people without knowledge. He wants the hand of the enemy exposed. The enemy is bold in what he does, cunning, and crafty. But God will make a way of escape if we listen.

It can be the same for the brothers. There have some brothers who have lost good jobs, gotten tied up with women who rob them of their peace of mind, paying child support, worrying about his kids because he didn't know the mother didn't take care of her other children so what would make her be any different with the child he had with her.

I can go on with many more stories, but what I want to share is God wants you free from bondage externally and internally. The Bible tells us there is "nothing new under the sun." There is a Bible story I encourage you to read. It is most known as *The Parable of the Lost Son* (Luke 15:11-32). This young man wanted his independence and he did not want to wait.

"There was a man who had two sons. The younger one said to his father, 'Father, give me my share of the estate.' So, he divided his property between them and the young man left his father's house.

Being independent was not like the young man thought it would be. Life was nothing like he wanted. However, the good news is God knows we will make mistakes and bad choices. The young man recognized the bad choice he made. He knew it was better at home. He did not let pride keep him from humbling himself and going home. His father eagerly welcomed him home just like God welcomes his children back into his arms when we have strayed.

While we are trying to be independent let's hope it teaches us patience and balance in our lives so that we don't keep falling and making bad choices. One of the sad things to me is being in situations and not learning from them. God wants us to be teachable and to have wisdom to help us in life's journeys. Proverbs 2:6 NIV, "For the Lord gives wisdom; from his mouth come knowledge and understanding."

There is nothing wrong with wanting to be independent, but ask yourself *what am I trying to be independent from.* I believe, as parents, we try to keep our children safe from making bad choices like we did, but we don't tell them why

> "If any man lacks wisdom, you should ask God, who gives generously to all without finding fault and it will be given to you" James 1:5 NIV

we feel the way we feel. We use our authority as a parent. If I could go back and change the time and the decisions I made back then without giving an explanation to my children, I would do that. Unfortunately, I cannot go back, but I can share the wisdom I have now. I wish someone would have been there to help me along the way. Most of all, I wish I would have had the knowledge to know God was with me all along.

Life brings many regrets. You cannot go back and change them, but you can learn from them and make your life better. Give God all your baggage of past mistakes. Watch him move on your behalf and welcome you back just like the father welcomed back his prodigal son. God loves you. He wants what is best for you and for me. That is why I need him because I can't do this thing called life without Him.

Let us pray:

Father, thank you for letting us have independence in the perfect balance. Help us to understand we need someone in our lives to bring balance. We need You to help us bring balance and structure, healing, power, love, correction, victory and so much more. We need you to heal us. For those of us who are broken, make us whole. Heal those of us who believe we have it all together.

You are the source of our strength. There is so much in us that keeps us bound. Free us from the need to be independent and then causes so much damage in our lives. Help us learn to wait and mature before stepping out the boat and into the water we call life. Let us be willing to not rush.

Do not let us spend and waste our inheritance or give it away only to find it brings no return. Help us to find wisdom and understanding through Your Word and allow us to be established and rooted in the Word. Help us to see traps and snares that the enemy has set for us and help us to hear your voice. Go before us and make the crooked places straight.

Thank you for watching over us when we made bad choices and decisions. Thank you for keeping us in our mistakes and shortcomings. Build us up to be that which you called us to be while trying to become or stay independent. Give us what we need to become balanced and complete in all areas of our lives. In Jesus' name. Amen.

Ask God to remove anything that is not like Him. Write down the things you want Him to change in your life.

_____

_____

_____

_____

_____

_____

_____

_____

_____

_____

_____

_____

_____

_____

_____

_____

_____

_____

_____

_____

Why Am I Lonely?

Loneliness has long been viewed as a universal condition which, at least to a moderate extent, is felt by everyone. Wikipedia defines loneliness as *an unpleasant emotional response to perceived isolation.* That is a mouthful by itself, but we have experienced loneliness in marriage, around others, and even with family. I believe some of us bring loneliness on ourselves because we are not friendly, perhaps because of things that happened in our lives or you may just be *introverted.*

The Bible talks about us when we bring it upon ourselves. Proverbs 18:24 KJV, "A man that hath friends must shew himself friendly: and there is a friend that sticketh closer than a brother."

I have a child that is *different* and apparently has caused trauma to others because of not being friendly. Grown folks have asked me what's wrong with her or what's her problem.

My child said, "Why do grown people need *me* to say hello to make *them* feel better?"

Not to say it was right but their validation should not be a child's responsibility to fill. Ok, I admit it was a ministry dealing with her until God gave me the revelation. I guess my friends and family expected her to be like me, but she is *not* me. For instance, and unlike my daughter, I will go out of my way to make sure I give you what you need to be ok with me, and she is the opposite.

Sometimes we are lonely due to our choices. My child chose to want to be left alone. I stopped trying to force her to be like me and she turned out fine. When she wants to socialize, she socializes with family, friends, and her church family. She loves to travel and work. She has come a long way and doing better but I'm sure God is not finished with her, or us, yet.

A person can be lonely in a marriage. In my marriage, I was being abused. I pulled away and it felt like I was alone. I no longer wanted to be with him or around him. He was also cheating on me. I didn't want to be caught up in drama. I never was good at putting on acts for people. So, I just kept to myself or with family and my real friends.

Some might think that it is impossible to be married and still be lonely, but it happens more often than people think. I'm sure there are many people with this same or similar story. I never thought I would be in that type of marriage, but I don't blame him for everything. I made the choice to marry him against my mother's wishes. If I had listened, I would have saved myself a lot of trouble. I don't regret my past anymore. It is behind me and that is where it will stay.

You cannot change the past, but you can learn from your mistakes. Never be in a place where you can't accept your responsibility in your life choices. Don't end up angry, bitter, and lonely because of not letting others in after bad relationships. I was not going to be old with cats when I could have chosen to love and trust again. Instead, of being lonely because of heartbreak or trust issues the Bible says we are to forgive so we may be forgiven because unforgiveness will settle in when we regret our choices.

Matthew 6:14 NIV, "For if you forgive other people when they sin against you, your heavenly Father will also forgive you."

Sometimes, and it may be while you are in church, you may not feel like you fit in. For me, I know it's more me than it is others. That is something I must become more aware of. If you find yourself in a same or similar state, own it and become aware of it so you can be free from the spirit of loneliness.

Next, loneliness can cause you to make decisions that are not the best choice for you. It could be because you get bored easily and you don't want to be bothered with people nor do you have real concern for others. But this goes against the Word of God.

Jesus said, "Thou shalt love the Lord God with your whole heart and with thy whole soul, and with thy whole mind: and

the second like this: thou shalt love thy neighbor as thyself"
(Matthew 22 37-39 KJV).

So, if you are choosing to be lonely by choice or by pain
you need to be set free. Genesis 2:18 NIV talks about men
should not be alone. That is why Eve was brought forth.
"The Lord God said, "It is not good for the man to be alone. I
will make a helper suitable for him." Ecclesiastes 4:9 NLT,
"Two people are better off than one, for they can help each
other succeed." So, despite me feeling that way I learned that I
am never alone, but God is always with me. When I have the
feeling of loneliness I can cast it down in Jesus' name.

Please do not be stuck or choose loneliness when it tries to
come on you. Instead, seek the Word. If you are without
family or friends, in a place of heartbreak, or whatever the
reason is know God is always with you. If you have a church
home, seek out Christian fellowship but let God lead you.
Also, in your family He normally gives you someone to be in
contact with but do not let your introverted issues get in your
way.

There are other things that cause loneliness such as, loss of
loved ones, loss of jobs, broken relationships, sickness and so
much more. But God has a plan for your life and loneliness is
not a part of it.

There are times when God wants to minister to us and we
may be drawn to His presence. We need each other. We need
pastors to bring the message, evangelists for correction,
apostles for foundation, teachers to teach, prophets to see,
people to keep us in line, and brothers and sisters for
fellowship .Our natural family is the same. We need fathers to
protect and teach, mothers to nurture, brothers and sisters for
fun and encouragement, and grandparents to override the mom
and dad.

Do not let loneliness win in your life. We all need
someone. Know that God loves you. He wants what is best for
you. If you have family and friends, they love you too. Do not
let the enemy tell you anything different. God will put
someone in your path, but you must be open to it and know it
is of God.

Sometimes we see an older couple and when their spouse passes on the remaining person becomes lonely and passes away soon after. If that void of loneliness is not filled, mainly in couples that have been together for over 25 years, their hearts are full of loss. If there are no children it is even more common. We need God to help us make it through our emotional highs and lows.

I pray that this will enlighten you to come out of loneliness and live your life to the fullest in Christ. He has so much more for us. He wants you and me to live life, love, and trust, find joy, peace, and have victory in every area.

Let us pray:

Father, help us to defeat the spirit of loneliness. No matter what the cause, it doesn't matter. Help us see you have so much more for us. Let us find joy, peace, and love again.

Father, allow us to see that two are better than one. Help us find the people you have called to be in our life. Give us wisdom to choose better. Let the past stay in the past and help us to move forward. Heal our hearts and lives again and defeat any spirit of loneliness. Help us to work on our social skills and to try to be a people person. Help us to make good friends and to call or text family and friends.

Lord, help us be the person You have called us to be. We cannot do it alone. We give You our will and we pray for others who are battling with the spirit of loneliness. Set them free too. For those who are not saved, bring salvation and give them understanding and peace to obtain victory.

Father, cover our minds and thoughts. We pray this prayer in Jesus' name. Amen.

Take a moment and submit your personal prayers to Him.

_____
_____
_____
_____
_____

Why Am I Unable To Leave?

Sometimes we find ourselves stuck or stagnated in a particular situation or relationship. I want to touch on it briefly. I found myself stuck in a couple of places, not just in my marriage but with family, friendships, relationships, in jobs, even in ministry. But the most dangerous place I was stuck in was my mindset.

Once I make up my mind about something it is hard for me to change it. But everything changes with time. It can be hard for some to change their thought process, depending on the person's upbringing or what you have been taught.

For example, racism is taught. A person is not born with racism in their mind and heart. Different beliefs and lifestyles are taught, picked up, or chosen. In sexual privies you are not born with certain tendencies. Why? Because God said He made *male* and *female*. Some of you may say God changed his mind but Numbers 23:19 NIV says, "God is not like human, that he should lie, not a human being that he changes his mind. Does he speak and then not act? Does he promise and not fulfill?"

> Genesis 5:2 also in Mark 10:6 NLT "But 'God made them male and female' from the beginning of creation.

If you are a believer this is what God says. If you are a non-believer this is still what God says. I am not judging or condemning you or your life choices. I have no heaven or hell to send you to, but God does and judgment will come to everyone.

The mindset we pick up from parents and family, our environment, and teachings is very impactful in our lives. We must seek God and the Bible to renew our minds. The Bible is true.

I thought I was doing great until I learned the Word of God. I was living wrong and didn't even know it. When I came into the knowledge of the Word, I had to do something different. I was living with the person I loved. Life was good. I had no complaints until I found out I was fornicating in God's sight.

I was not tithing and my money seemed like I had holes in my pockets just like it says in Haggai 1:6 NIV, "You have planted much, but harvest little you eat but never have enough, you drink, but never have you fill. You put on clothes but are never warm. You earn wages only to put them in a purse with holes in it."

I could go all day with things that enlighten me by reading the Word of God. I am trying to give wisdom and not judgment. I have been in a lot of wrong places and I have made a bunch of bad decisions but when I came into the knowledge of the Word it was up to me to change.

No one can tell you what to do. God won't go against your will nor will I. We all believe differently so please do not get offended. Just try him for yourself.

There was someone I knew who was in an adulterous relationship for a long time. He took good care of her and she loved him, but she also knew God. She told me she was going to leave him, and that she knew what they were doing was wrong; but nothing changed. Soon, the more I went to visit her, the more she confided in me. She started asking me to pray for her and, then *with* her.

Over a long period, she was finally ready to walk away. That was not easy, especially when a person is taking care of you and she had been with him for 10 or more years. But she finally made the move. She stopped taking his money, moved away, and got her own apartment.. She asked me to help her walk through the process.

I had been in an abusive marriage that I stayed in for way too long. I told her what God said, which was *how can I give you what you deserve, if you won't let go of what you have.* Often, we cry out for change but we won't trust God in or through the process.

When my friend ended the adulterous affair, she met and started dating a pastor. Within probably a year after meeting him, they were married and she became a First Lady.

Sometimes we don't know or understand why we stay in a bad relationship. Sometimes we think about the time we invested in it. You may think you can't do any better or that this is the year that things will change. We don't see that we are in a dysfunctional relationship.

When I was trying to get out of my former relationship, it seemed like something traumatic would happen and we would stay together to support one another. This happened until the Holy Spirit revealed it was over no matter what happened. This is just a thought to think on for a few minutes. God created us. Don't you think He knows what's best for us.

I don't believe life always has to be bad for you to be stuck. You may have a decent relationship or job but what if you are made for more?

I'll end this by saying again, wisdom is learned. Doing right is hard sometimes, and believing for better almost doesn't existent. You have settled and compromised long enough. It is time to reach your full potential in life. I am just touching on a few things in our lives that keep us back. Do not stay in dead-in relationships, jobs, ministries, neighborhoods, family traditions, or religion. Get out and do what God is saying and receive what God has for you. 3 John 1:2 KJV says, "Beloved I wish above all things that thou mayest prosper and be in health even as thy soul prospereth."

He wants us to renew our minds. Romans 12:2 NIV, "Do not conform to the pattern of this world. but be transformed by the renewing of the mind, then will you be able to test and approve what God's will is; his good, pleasing and perfect will."

My friend who is now First Lady had to renew her mind to get what God had for her. To God be the glory.

God wants each of us to choose Him, but it is a choice we all must make for ourselves. God wants us to choose Him so we can have life and have it abundantly, but we must let go of what we have first. It's like holding 100 dollars in your hand with your fist tight and someone keeps telling you to open your hand and let it go in exchange for what they have in their hand. Because you don't know what they have you weigh your odds. They could be holding a dollar. I do understand, but God is not like man. He would never tell you to let go unless He has something better. He knows the thoughts He thinks toward you. Those thoughts are good and not evil.

This is why I need Him to help me get out of the wrong mindset so I can live according to His Word and His purpose for my life.

Let us pray:

Father, thank you for releasing me out of bad relationships, dead end jobs, family traditions, religious ways, ministries that you have not placed me in, and bad decisions that have kept me in places I should have left. You said you would give me a way of escape. So, Father my trust and hope is in you. Give me wisdom and renew my mind.

Lord, I need your guidance and Your Word to bring forth the person you have called me to be, not what the world has said. I want the things you have chosen for me. Deliver me, renew in me a right spirit, and create in me a clean heart. Father, not my will but Your will be done in my life.

Help me to know You have more and better for me. Teach me to let go and to trust You. Get me out of a false mindset and bring me to the reality of who You called me to be. Help me to let go of those things that easily bind me. I cannot do it without You. I cannot find true victory, peace, love, joy, truth, wisdom, understanding, hope, healing, and deliverance without You. In Jesus' name. Amen.

Take a moment to pray, and then write down what you need and want from God.

_____
_____
_____
_____
_____
_____
_____

Stacy Rhodes

Why Am I Unable to Stay?

There are some people who want to leave a situation or relationship but they do not know how to leave. Others may be in a good relationship but choose not to stay. This can happen in personal relationships and also in relationships on the job, in the church, and even in church ministry.

Some of us jump from place to place, relationship to relationship, job to job, one church to the next. The Word of God says in James 1:8 KJV, "A double-minded person is unstable in his ways." I have known double-minded people. They change their minds a lot and are unstable in all they do. If you listen closely, even in conversation, they are all over the place. Thanks to God for giving me wisdom. I see a lot clearer now. Many have blown good relationships because of cheating and committing adultery. Many of these same people will say they love the person who they are in a relationship with but for some reason they just cannot stop cheating on their spouse or significant other. They are satisfying their lusts. There are people who had great jobs, careers, and opportunities and they walked away from it all.

"For though we walk in the flesh, we are not waging war according to the flesh. For the weapons of our warfare are not of the flesh but have divine power to destroy strongholds" (2 Corinthians 10:3-4 ESV).

God has given us the proper tools to bring down these generational curses that are running rampant through our bloodlines. This must stop NOW. We can bring an end to it through prayer, fasting, and obtaining the knowledge of truth.

There are many women who believe *all* men want to cheat and jump from relationship to relationship. I don't exactly agree. You see, I believe sometimes they are fighting against things they cannot see. Maybe they have been hurt, broken and are ashamed, angry, or feel guilty. Maybe they have insecurities attached to their past. Yet, we often believe what they did (i.e., cheating, walking away from relationships) was intentional. Sometimes this is true, but most times it's not. Men, I am not bashing you. I know women who are the same. They refuse to commit. They had good men in their corner, but they walked away for many of the same reasons.

I have been in a relationship where the man gave me his money, his time, his car, and the shirt off his back if I wanted it, but his ability to commit to me was hard, literally impossible. As I look back on it now, it wouldn't have worked anyway with us. He would have felt forced to commit to a deadline of marrying me. Ladies and men, if you have to force someone to marry you by giving them ultimatums and deadlines, you *should* walk away. If *you* don't walk away, the other person should walk away. The world calls this *cold feet* or being *unable to commit*. God calls it double-mindedness. Remember, if someone loves you they will make that commitment without force.

In friendships, you have some friends playing both sides. They may be friends with you while also being friends with a person they know you dislike. They jump from one idea to the next, without doing any of it. One day they may say they want a storefront business and the next day they want a home-based business. Their ideas shift like the wind. I have seen this happen in ministry. Someone in the ministry says God told them to do street ministry one day and the next day God told them to open a church.

People, God is *not* fickle; nor does He *change* his mind like that. We should not be fickle like that either. The Bible says "But let your communication be Yea, yea or Nay, nay for whatsoever is more than these comes from the evil one" Matthew 5:37 KJV.

Do not let being double-mindedness slip in. None of us is exempt. It can be doing something as simple as shopping. You are already behind in bills. You know you do not need another pair of shoes, purse or sneakers, yet you go shopping and buy stuff anyway. Now you're worried and frustrated trying to play catch-up on bills.

The enemy knows our weaknesses. He will use those weaknesses against us to make us double-minded in different areas of our lives, including friendships and relationships. Some of you are in and out of relationships and friendships and you already know you are going to be hurt once again. Yet you go back, leave, and go back again. So, for the ones who cannot commit, now you are wavering in your final decision. That is a spirit of double-mindedness running rampant in you. Something is easier to see when you are no longer tied to it. This is why you need to take some time to heal when coming out of a relationship or bad situation. Believe me, it took a long time for me to get to this point in my life. To God be the glory. I can go back any minute if I start depending on me instead of depending on God.

If you are reading this and you are that person who can't stay or commit, God wants you to search yourself. He wants you to find the root cause of why you are this way. It can be more than double-mindedness, but trust me, double-mindedness *is* one of the causes.

For those who are dealing with these type of people make sure you have a prayer life and a Word from God because it is no easy task. You can end up devastated, broken, bitter, angry, in doubt, trying to figure why you were never *good enough* for the double-minded person.

It has nothing to do with you; and everything to do with their own issues. My advice to you is to get yourself free. This advice is for the double-minded person as well as the person who is dealing with a double-minded type of person.

> "I know thy works, that thou art neither cold nor hot: I would thou wert cold or hot. So then because thou art lukewarm, and neither cold nor hot, I will spue thee out of my mouth" (Revelations 3: 15-16 KJV).

Again, this is not just a male thing. I have seen women who couldn't commit and who bounce around in relationships. But remember, this is not of God. He does not like it. Clearly, He wants us to make a decision so we are not being deceived or double-minded.

Staying in a relationship requires commitment, sacrifice, compromising with balance, patience, and humility. When we are double-minded those words are not in our thinking. That is why if the person is double-minded staying in a relationship and/or situation is not an option. Do not always blame the other person, but use wisdom. Learn about the people in your life. You can save your emotions and feelings. Stop jumping in relationships so fast. No matter what kind of relationship it is, stop letting people have your whole heart. Do not give them access to things they did not earn in your life for them only to leave you broken and disappointed.

For me, once I released myself from this relationship, I was able to guard my heart likes the Bible tells us to do. I learned why it says that through God given wisdom. Proverbs 4:23 NIV says, "Above all guard your heart for everything you do flows from it."

I now have the understanding that when my heart is hurting it contaminates everything else in my life. I'm sure you have seen, known, or been hurt and you can't get past it. Or, perhaps you are still stuck over an offense that happened 20-years ago. After all this time, you are still angry, mean, and nasty about it like it just happened yesterday.

I don't know about you, but I would rather walk in the victory God has called me to walk in. You too, can learn how to commit and find love, peace, joy, and how to trust and not be double-minded. You do not want to be blowing like the wind. You want to be planted by the water, make good choices, and have a firm foundation. This is God's will for our lives, that we come into the knowledge of Him and His Word.

My ability to *stay* got better with the Word and through prayer. I learned how to commit, how to deal with my issues, and how to recognize that which was not mine to handle. This is why I need Him…so do you.

Let us pray:

Father, thank you that we are not being double-minded in our decision making, in our daily lives, in our walk with you, on our jobs, in our businesses, in raising our children, in our marriages and relationships.

Thank you that our yea will be yea and our nay will be nay. Let us not be lukewarm. We do not want you to spit us out. We want to draw closer to You, Father, and have a better spirit of discernment. We want to be stable in our choices, in our walk, in our families, in our marriages, in our healing, in our relationships, and in our entire lives. Let our trust and hope be in You. Help our loved ones, our friends, our neighbors, and our church family.

Father, thank you that You are God and God alone. You are in whom we trust. You are the only one who can help us to obtain wisdom and the knowledge of truth found in Your Word.

Let us walk in the spirit and not after the flesh. Lead and guide us into all truth. We need You more than we ever did. Show up and be our light in this dark world, for our hope, trust, and deliverance is in You. We pray this prayer in Jesus' name. Amen.

If you are one of the persons who can't *stay*, I encourage you to pray and ask God to help you get free from double-mindedness and anything else that hinders you. God can and will set you free. Write down your prayers and those things you want God to deliver you from so you will not be walking around as a double-minded person.

_____
_____
_____
_____
_____
_____
_____
_____
_____
_____
_____
_____
_____
_____
_____

Stacy Rhodes

Why Am I Unable To Break My Addictions?

According to Google online, one of the main definitions for *addiction* (paraphrased) is "the fact or condition of being addicted to a particular substance, thing or activity or an inability to some using substance or engaging in a behavior that becomes compulsive and often continues despite harmful consequences."

I will touch on this subject according to what God has shown me. I remember praying and asking God, "God, how can I minister about something I haven't done or experienced?" God's answer to me was I could minister about it because I have lived with those who have been addicted.

I started thinking about when I was a youngster and my family would be drinking. When the whiskey bottle got low that's when the fighting started. Hot grease and whatever else my family could get their hands on were used as weapons. Just about every weekend someone had to go to the hospital.

As I grew up, I told myself there would be no drinking for me. Because of the things I saw drinking could do to destroy families and people, I wanted no part of it. Unfortunately, most of my family didn't follow my path. I learned early on what a drinking addiction comes with because I saw my family suffer deeply from it. Drinking turned into them taking drugs.

Drugs were 10 times worst in my sight. I had family members who were ready to do any and everything just to get their hands on drugs and more drugs. I have seen addiction destroy relationships, families, marriages, children, and the addict's health. It was heartbreaking to see them living in abandoned houses because of their addiction. Finding them in bad situations and trying to get them out of it but it fails. Some families step up to take care of the drug addicts' children while they run the streets, and steal from your home to supply their habits. You watch them lose everything chasing drugs and drinking. Smoking is usually wrapped up in these addictions too. I don't see how people do it; I don't like the smell of cigarettes or weed. I take no credit but I believe God had His hand on my life. That was just from my eyes. I can't imagine what their real stories are.

There can be shame and guilt that comes when the addict wakes up out of their drug addiction. I have seen people get clean only to fall back into using drugs again. I asked God what makes them want to stay in something like that. Some were chasing it because they liked it. Some got hooked because they thought they were stronger than the drug. Others have pains they are trying to run from and others may have had it forced on them.

Those addicted to sex are looking for love, pleasure, and power. It can be like a drug too because you want more and more. If not, careful you can start drifting into perverted sex such as pornography, swinging, and homosexuality. It is all a set up from the enemy.

Shopping and eating can be addictions. These are dangerous too. It can put you in debt because you are constantly buying stuff you don't need and can't afford, or you're eating so much that your weight has doubled and your body can't carry the weight, so then your heart can't function properly, and there goes clogged arteries. Plus smoking harms your lungs. You think you're only hurting yourself, but that is not true. If you have people who love you, they share in your pain and are worried about you. The Word talks about us being enticed by our own lust.

"He who loves pleasures will become a poor man: He who loves wine and oil will not become rich." Proverbs 21:17 NASB

James 1:14 CJB, "Rather each person is being tempted whenever he is being dragged off and enticed by the bait of his own desire."

Addiction can make you anxious but God tells us to *be anxious for nothing*. Addiction is real but so is God. People can be delivered, but the first thing is to admit you have a problem. Second--seek help. Third--do not try to do it alone. Breaking an addiction is not easy so you need help. Do it God's way. Get help, seek prayer and pray in agreement for deliverance. I believe in some cases deliverance and professional help are needed at the same time. Nevertheless, trust and know that God is able to clean you up and turn you around. It is not His will for you to remain in your addictions. Here are some scriptures to read and meditate on.

Romans 12:2 NIV, "Do not conform to the pattern of this world, but be transformed by the renewing of your mind. Then you will be able to test and approve what God's will is—his good, pleasing and perfect will."

John 10:10 NIV, "The thief comes only to steal and kill and destroy; I have come that they may have life, and have it to the full."

Galatians 5:1NIV, "It is for freedom that Christ has set us free. Stand firm, then, and do not let yourselves be burdened again by a yoke of slavery."

2 Timothy 4:18 NIV, "The Lord will rescue me from every evil attack and will bring me safely to his heavenly kingdom. To him be glory for ever and ever. Amen."

Romans 6:14 NIV, "For sin shall no longer be your master, because you are not under the law, but under grace."

Psalm 50:15 NIV, "And call on me in the day of trouble; I will deliver you, and you will honor me."

These are just a few scriptures for you to study and meditate on. If you cry out to God, He is able to set you free, and who He sets free is free indeed.

> "The righteous cry out, and the Lord hears them; he delivers them from all their troubles." Psalm 34:17 NIV

Some of you may need to go through the 12 Steps Program or enter a rehabilitation facility. You may need meds to help you get clean. I'm not knocking this nor am I saying you don't need this. What I am saying is if you know Christ, please try Him too. I have seen Him bring deliverance and victory to those who have a relationship with Him and stay in His presence through prayer and fellowship.

Do not let the enemy have you believing you cannot get out of addiction. God will and can set you free, but you must trust and believe He is able to deliver you and bring you through. It is not His will that you should perish or be bound to addictions. He wants you to walk in wisdom and stand on the Word for your life. He can bring you out of darkness and into His marvelous light. If you call on Him, He will answer, if you just believe.

If you do not know God, you can invite Him into your life right now by asking Him to become your Lord and savior. "If you confess with your mouth and believe in your heart that God raised Jesus from the dead, you will be saved" (Romans 10:9). Welcome into the family of Christ. Find a church home so you can learn the Word and hear a message from God.

Every day is a new challenge in Christ. This is why I need him. You will as well. We need strength to break addictions and strongholds. We need God to get us through the bad times. We need support from family, friends, and the church because habits are easy to start but hard to break.

I have watched my sister struggle with addiction her whole adult life. I wish she could see what I see and what God sees in her. I see the purpose on her life. God sees the plans He had for her life. He has given us power over all things. That includes addictions of all kinds. Speak the Word and pray. You can follow the addiction programs but take God with you.

Addiction has destroyed many lives, caused much shame and guilt, broken marriages, torn apart families, made people lose jobs, homes, and much more. But we shall go into the enemy's camp and take back what belongs to God. We will preach the gospel and the good news. We will lay hands and ask God for deliverance and healing. For God is a waymaker, a miracle worker, and a promise keeper. He is light in the darkness. He will keep us from the hand of the enemy. He will deliver us from the enemy too. This is why I need him. This is why you should know that you need him too.

Let us pray:

Father, thank you for deliverance from all forms of addictions. We ask you to clean us up and deliver us from all situations that do not mean us any good.

Lord, take away urges and the taste of drugs, heroin, cocaine, opioids, meth, molly, alcohol, porn, food, shopping addiction, sexual thoughts and urges, cigarettes, weed, hookah, thrill-seeking, everything that was not named. Help us to break these habits . Bring us back to who we were and are meant to be before we started.

Lord, help us to defeat our addictions and get our lives back. Restore everything the enemy has stolen from us. Remove guilt, shame, and brokenness. Deliver us from the root cause of our addictions. Heal us and make us whole in You.

You said if we call on You, You will answer us. We need You. We don't want to bring peace to our families and restore broken relationships. Remove any and all hurt we caused others and ourselves. Restore our damaged bodies brought about during our time of addiction.

Forgive us for stealing and hurting our loved ones and anyone else we hurt. Help us to forgive ourselves as well.

Father, turn our ashes into beauty. Exchange the garment of heaviness for a garment of praise. We rebuke you Satan out of our thoughts.

Father God, renew in us a right spirit. Create in us a clean heart. In Jesus' name. Amen.

Take a moment to write down what you need God to do in your Life.

_____
_____
_____
_____
_____
_____
_____
_____
_____
_____
_____
_____
_____

Stacy Rhodes

Why Am I Unable to See My Faults?

Many times we go around blaming others for things they have no control over. Sometimes we blame God for our bad choices and life situations. We all have them, but we do not see clearly when we are in pain, hurt, angry, bitter or resentful. Unforgiveness of these things can cloud our thoughts and bring disruption to our lives.

You are probably wondering why I am always focused on these things. The answer is because these things I listed are our enemy just as much as a murderer, kidnapper, and child molester. With so much hurt throughout our lives, broken promises, relationships, and friendships we may have a hard time forgiving or seeing our own faults and the role we played in some of the things that happened in our lives.

I talk about my abusive marriage, but I rarely talk about the part when I said *I do* to him. Therefore, I take some of the blame and responsibility for saying *I do* to the marriage. Many times in my life I could have made better decisions. I made so many decisions based upon my flesh or my emotions. I think back over my life. When I got saved and in the Word I wasn't so quick to make fleshly decisions anymore. It was a check in my spirit so I thought things through more. I thank God for His wisdom. I thank Him for His son Jesus and for His Word.

> "For the flesh desires what is contrary to the Spirit, and the Spirit what is contrary to the flesh. They are in conflict with each other, so that you are not to do whatever you want."
> Galatians 5:17 NIV

In Ephesians 2:3 NASB "For speaking out arrogant words of vanity they entice by fleshly desires, by sensuality, those who barely escape from the ones who live in error."

When we try to help ourselves and self-teach ourselves, we can sink deeper into our mess. I have come to learn that I am not my best teacher. Most of the time, I cannot see when I am in error. My faults will always be minimum in my sight. I know it is not easy accepting responsibility when you are wrong or at fault. But as you grow in God it will get easier.

James 5:16 KJV reminds us to, "Confess your faults one to another, and pray one for another, that ye may be healed. The effectual fervent prayer of a righteous man availeth much."

Many times we do not listen and so we fail to see the error of our ways. Sometimes you can rebel so much that you become blind to your faults and shortcomings. You don't want to see or acknowledge them. You would rather stay in self-pity and allow the enemy to minister to you instead of God.

When you do this, you cannot see your faults. You wish you could change things but regret and guilt keep you bound. You blame others for you not being along further in life, when the truth is if they were not holding you hostage you still stayed willingly, making it a mutual decision.

> "All scripture is given by inspiration of God, and is profitable for doctrine, for reproof, for correction, for instruction in righteousness."
> 2 Timothy 3:16 KJV

Our faults are not always immediately noticed, and that is okay, because once again God looked beyond our faults and saw we had a need so He sent his son to help us get the victory.

We must start listening to God and learning the Word. Proverbs 3:5-6 KJV tells us, "Trust in the Lord with all thine heart; and lean not unto thine own understanding. In all thy ways acknowledge him, and he shall direct thy paths."

The Word of God is what helps us keep ourselves in order, plus mentors, counselors, friends, parents, grandparents, and different other forms of authority.

One of the many things I love about the Lord is He looked beyond our faults and saw we had a need for a savior. God is simply amazing. This is why I give Him praise. He has made it so you and I never have to be alone.

John 14:6 KJV, "Jesus saith unto him, I am the way, the truth, and the life: no man cometh unto the Father, but by me."

Accepting Jesus as my Lord and Savior is the best decision I ever made. He delivered me, healed me, saved me, brought me into His light, and set me free when I was bound. He has been there for me in so many ways. I am truly grateful. I want to shout from the rooftops and tell of His goodness. I am ready to tell my story and give You the glory, Lord. I am ready to surrender. I am ready to end these sleepless nights and to do what is right by You, Lord. Your only son paid the price by laying down his life.

In Luke 4:18 KJV, "The Spirit of the Lord is upon me, because he hath anointed me to preach the gospel to the poor; he hath sent me to heal the brokenhearted, to preach deliverance to the captives, and recovering of sight to the blind, to set at liberty them that are bruised."

God loves you. He wants to bring you out and open your eyes so you can see your faults and your strengths. Once you *see*, He can bring you through. God knows you will share your testimony with others. So, get free and start sharing the good news. Remember, He will be with you always even until the end. If God be for you who can stand against you. This is why I need Him. I want to see clearer. I want to become better for Him, myself, and others. I want to stop fault finding and take responsibility for me.

Let us pray:

Father, thank you for eyes to see ourselves and our faults. Thank you for helping us to become better in seeing and hearing what the spirit has to say. Lord, we are in places we put ourselves in, but we repent and ask you to forgive us. Deliver us and set us free from bad choices. Let us cling to that which is good and walk away from all that is evil and bad. Help us not to see the spec in our brother or sister's eye but help us to remove the beam in ours. we need you to keep us focused and help us make responsible choices. Help us walk in newness of sight, give us a spirit of discernment, set us free from the bondage of sin.

Father, remove past hurts, heartbreaks, grief, depression, unforgiveness, bitterness, envy, strife, sickness, and anything that will open the door that leads to blindness. Help us keep our minds set on you. Keep our thoughts under control. Bring healing to our lives.

Father, you are great and greatly to be praised. Cover us. We will give you glory, honor, and praise. In Jesus' name. Amen.

Ask God to show you your faults so you can get free. Write down things you need Him to change.

_____

_____

_____

_____

_____

_____

_____

_____

_____

_____

_____

_____

_____

_____

_____

_____

_____

_____

_____

_____

_____

_____

_____

_____

Why Am I Educated but Without Knowledge

I don't have a college degree, but I know education is powerful and amazing. I speak, write, and talk from wisdom. God, the creator, has given me knowledge through the Holy Spirit. I used to tell God that I couldn't speak on certain things because I didn't know about it. God said different because I learned the Word of God is true. He says in His Word that the Holy Spirit will teach us and guide us.

> "But the Comforter, which is the Holy Ghost, whom the Father will send in my name, he shall teach you all things, and bring all things to your remembrance, whatsoever I have said unto you." John 14 :26 KJV

Matthew 10:19-20 CEB: "Whenever they hand you over, don't worry about how to speak or what you will say, because what you can say will be given to you at that moment. You aren't doing the talking, but the Spirit of my Father is doing the talking through you."

Luke 12:12 NIV: "For the Holy Spirit will teach you at that time what you should say." God has done this for me in a couple instances. The Word is alive and always active. I have seen wisdom working in my life. There were times when I didn't know what to say and the Holy Spirit spoke through me. This is why I say to you, change your form of thinking so it aligns with the Word. My life could have been so much different if I had known what I know now and what I have learned through the Word of God. This is why I am sharing this with you.

Education can help you to excel in the world. It can help you obtain spiritual knowledge so you can reach the goals for your life. According to American educational psychologist, David Krathwohl (May 14, 1921– October 13, 2016), there are four types of knowledge. They are factual, conceptual, procedural, and metacognitive. I'm not going that deep to explain what each type means. Feel free to research it for yourself. What I will say is how God defines knowledge.

Proverbs 1:7 NIV tells us, "The fear of the LORD is the beginning of knowledge, but fools despise wisdom and instruction."

Proverbs 2:10 NIV says, "For wisdom will enter your heart, and knowledge will be pleasant to your soul."

Proverbs 15:14 KJV: "The heart of him that hath understanding seeketh knowledge: but the mouth of fools feedeth on foolishness."

God showed me you can be educated but do not use all knowledge. We all think on different levels and obtain knowledge differently. Yet, to have an education but still fill empty lets you know that you are missing something. If you are that person, God wants you to draw closer to Him and obtain knowledge from the Word of God. He wants you to that knowledge to your life.

> "An intelligent heart acquires knowledge, and the ear of the wise seeks knowledge."
> Proverbs 18:15 ESV

You can have the knowledge to cook but not like cooking. You can be passed down gifts and talents but you do not use them because it is not your passion. I am educated in the field of medical assistant and nail technology but I am in God's ministry, which is my passion.

Yes, I can be educated without knowledge because knowledge is also having experience. When I took the class in nail technology I had to do an externship, but that was the extent of it. I was pregnant and did not want to do anything during that time. I took the classes, obtained the knowledge, but with the intent *not* to use it. I graduated at the top of my class. I believed in giving my all to whatever I did, which was something that was instilled in me.

I remember going to a church service where they were praying for those who were in school of who wanted to go back to school. I got in the prayer line. The pastors lined up to pray over each of us. As I stood before one of the pastors for prayer, she told me I would not be going to school because God said the Holy Spirit was going to be my teacher in all things. I did not know what that meant but I went and stood before the next pastor. This next pastor told me he didn't see me going to school. By this time, I was even more confused because I didn't understand why they would tell me that.

This was midpoint my walk with God so I was not trying to question them. I thought more about what the pastors said. They didn't mean I *couldn't* go to school so what I did was take a ministry course. All hell seemed to break loose while I was attending but I continued to give it my all. I excelled in the ministry course, but I tell you it was like pulling teeth to get it done. I am not a quitter so of course I finished but when I say everything but the kitchen sink was thrown at me, believe it.

I kept thinking what in the world was going on. I heard this scripture, "The blessing of the Lord makes a person rich without the painful toil in it" (Proverbs 10:22 KJV). I knew at that point I was out of His will. Since that time, I try to live my life through wisdom. As a result, I received understanding of the Word God spoken over my life.

What has been spoken over your life that you haven't received yet? I'm not putting down education or knowledge because both are needed. I am praying that you have received both, along with wisdom to live your life to the fullest.

I thank God He showed me how to share what He has taught me with others. I know what I say may not be for everyone, but he that have an ear let him hear what the spirit is saying.

Struggles you have can be less if you do it God's way. So as you get your education, get wisdom. As you obtain knowledge, get understanding. Apply it to your life. Do not be void of understanding. Do not be educated but without the knowledge of God.

When I came into the knowledge of Him my life got better. I am not knocking getting an education. I celebrate with you in all your accomplishments. I encourage every young person to finish school, go to college, take a trade, start a business and obtain knowledge that will help them. But along the journey, I cannot stress enough how important it is to pick up the Word of God too. Let the Holy Spirit lead and guide you into all truth.

I know it all has its rightful place, and I know some very well-educated people who also know God. I also know some successful, educated people who do not know Him.

| Education enhanced my knowledge, but gaining wisdom took it to a whole new level. |

I hope what I am sharing is helping you in your walk with God and helping you gain understanding and knowledge for your life. Do not feel bad if you do not excel like others, or you decide college isn't for you. Maybe you didn't finish high school. Ask God if you should you go back. He has a purpose and a plan for your life. He can use you where you are. It is for His glory and His perfect will for your life. Enjoy the ride and let God be God. This is why I need him...to bring me understanding.

I thank God for doctors, professors, nurses, scientists, lawyers, pastors, evangelists and so many other professions. I thank Him for education for without it where would we be. Without knowledge we would not have many of the things we have.

Kudos to you all but I give God the glory for creating it all and giving us knowledge to excel. God said let us make man in our image, after our likeness, so all things come from God. God says be it unto you according to your faith. Read Matthew 9 during your devotional time.

Let us pray:

Father, help us to know that the beginning of knowledge can help us to obtain education. Let knowledge and wisdom begin with the fear of You. Teach us so we can be full and without void so the enemy has no way in to push us off track. Wisdom will keep us focused on you. Help us to reach the level of education needed for each of us but do not let us be frustrated. When we do not excel like others and the enemy tells us we are stupid, dumb, or uneducated help us to focus on the Word which tells us we can do all things through Christ who strengthens us.

Father, guide us to obtain knowledge. Help us to use it to help others and ourselves. Thank you that we apply it to our lives. Give us wisdom so we can be blessed beyond measure.

Father, you are the source of our strength and the keeper of our minds. Shine down on us in our shortcomings and our inability to comprehend. Father, help us to be educated with knowledge and wisdom. In Jesus' name. Amen.

Write down what you need God to change in this area of your life.

_____
_____
_____
_____
_____
_____
_____
_____
_____
_____
_____
_____
_____
_____
_____
_____
_____
_____
_____
_____
_____
_____
_____

Why Am I Feeling Empty And Incomplete?

Have you ever felt empty in your life? Have there been times when you felt unfulfilled for no real reason? It can be explained as a void or empty space, like when your spirit feels incomplete. I was in this place when my sister passed away. I was there in the physical, but it was like I wasn't. I was functioning but was not feeling anything. Through the whole process I felt empty. I was functioning and staying strong for others, but she was my sister and my friend. I helped with the funeral; I talked with my family and supported them. I picked out flowers with my friend while feeling empty, with no emotions or feelings.

There was a void in my life when my sister died. I didn't know it then but I know now. I needed to be there for my family. In order for that to happen, I needed to withdraw my emotions which left me feeling empty. I cried at night when my kids and family were asleep or away. I felt the same void and emptiness when my niece passed away and again when my brother passed away last August. What kept me going and helped me to stay focused is worship, the Word of God, and sitting in God's presence.

I learned that God was the only thing that could fill that void of emptiness. He is the source of my strength, and I thank Him daily. When you get to that place, call on Him and He will answer you.

When I was young, my mom passed away. I experienced emptiness then as well. I put on my big girl pants and got it together. God allowed me to release my grief doing a service on my sister's birthday and later for my brother. I wasn't endowed with rivers of tears, but God gave me the moment I needed to be restored in that area.

> The Bible says in Isaiah 26:3 NIV, "You will keep in perfect peace those whose minds are steadfast, because they trust in you."

Have you ever been in that place of needing a refill from God when life has knocked you down, kicked you around, and thrown everything at you? Or you're in a place like the deer panting at the water for restoration. Some people do yoga and meditate. For me, prayer and worship allows me to get refilled in His presence.

God has showed up for you; He is not a respecter of persons. Find your place of restoration in the Lord. Ask Him to fill you up. When you fill empty, go into God's presence. Do not let your heart be troubled. God always has time for His children. He wants to restore us. "I was young and now I am old, yet I have never seen the righteous

> Isaiah 40:31 NIV:
> "But those who hope in the Lord will renew their strength. They will soar on wings like eagles; they will run and not grow weary, they will walk and not be faint."

forsaken or their children begging bread" (Psalm 37:25 NIV).

God is a good God. That is why I need Him to fill the void and emptiness in my life.

I remember trying to fix my life while trying to work my plans for me and my children. I thought I had it all together and that I didn't need anyone's help. I felt like everything was working out great. When my daughter got pregnant, I realized I couldn't do everything by myself. I recall this lady at my job named Emma (today I call her 'Mom').

One day I broke down at work and Emma invited me to church. I went because I knew I needed something in my life. It was the beginning of 1998. Since then I have never left God or Emma. But the greatest thing is God hasn't left me even after seeing all my faults and me getting off track. I know He loves me. He is so amazing. My relationship with Emma is still strong and she just turned 91 years old! I may have lost my mom a long time ago, but God replaced her with Emma.

It has been a long walk and I still have much to learn. I can assure you that God loves you too. He wants you to know it. My walk with God has made me complete in Him. Wisdom has made me see it. I can give you testimony after testimony of trials and tribulations that were real, and God brought me out. He set me free from bondages and delivered me from so many

Stacy Rhodes

things. He kept my family and loved ones. For me, I wasn't complete until I found God.

I tried so many things to be complete, but I have come to find that wholeness is what completion really is in Christ. We have seen the world chasing so many things and they are still not satisfied or complete. What is *right* the world labels it as *wrong*. But God's Word has already been established. He said in 2 Timothy 3:2 NIV "People will be lovers of themselves, lovers of money, boastful, proud, abusive, disobedient to their parents, ungrateful, unholy, without love, unforgiving, slanderous, without self-control, brutal, not lovers of the good."

So, we should not be shocked with the way the world is going. We should be made complete in God in James 1:4 CEB, "...let endurance have its perfect result, so that you may be perfect and complete, lacking nothing."

This is why I need Him—to be complete and made whole through Him. There is no greater feeling in this world than finding God. He shows you how to be healed and made whole. That brings completeness and fills every void. Keep learning and getting better through His love and through the Word.

Let us pray:

Father, we first want to ask you to fill the emptiness we experience. Fill every void in our lives. We need all those thoughts, issues, sicknesses, grief, depression, lack, and brokenness that draws us into those empty moments. Bring them under subjection to You.

You told us to cast our cares upon you for You care for us. So fill us up, Father. Help us to replace our emptiness with the Word which gives us strength, hope, joy, peace, patience, provision and so much more. Let us not forget Your benefits. Help us to be made whole in You. Draw us nearer unto You. Father, help us shift our way of thinking. Remove everything that is not like You. Make us whole and complete through Your Word.

Father, our hope is in You. Our trust is in You. Father, so many people need You. We pray for those who do not know You to come unto You. Save our loved ones. Save our enemies too. Let them draw closer to You. Save our country and our children. Let us find wisdom and peace. In Jesus' name. Amen.

Take a moment and talk with the Lord. Tell him where you feel empty. Ask Him to make you complete in Him.

_____

_____

_____

_____

_____

_____

_____

_____

_____

_____

_____

_____

_____

_____

_____

_____

_____

_____

_____

_____

_____

_____

_____

_____

_____

_____

_____

Why Do I Love Him?

I love the Lord. He is the keeper of my soul. He is the Lord God that heals. He is my rock, my fortress, my waymaker, and my promise keeper. He is a miracle worker, the Rose of Sharon, Lily of the Valley, Morning Star, the Great I Am, the Bread of life, Lord of Lords, and King of Kings. He is the Prince of Peace. He is Jehovah Jireh, Jehovah Nissi, Jehovah Rophe, Jehovah Shalom, Jehovah Yahweh, Jehovah Tireh, Jehovah N'Kaddesh, Jehovah Sabaoth, Jehovah Rohi, Jehovah Tsidkenu, Jehovah Shammah, Elohim, El Elyon, El-Shaddai, Adonai, but most of all He is love. He showed love toward us by giving His only son. I want to give it back to Him as the Bible tells us to do. I need God so I can learn how to love correctly.

My husband and I started as friends. We met, a bond was formed, and as we grew in life together our friendship and love grew until we became more than friends.

With God, I believed there was a God but I had to learn how to trust Him. I went to church to learn about him. From there, I learned how to spend

> The Bible tells us how to love God in Matthew 22:37 NIV. "Love the Lord your God with all your heart and with all your soul and with all your mind. This is the first and great commandment. The second is like unto, thou shall love thy neighbor as thyself."

time with Him and then came correction. I got deliverance by studying and learning God's way. I stayed in His presence, studied His Word, and found out who He is. I thought He was like a person I could see or touch daily, but as I grew with Him, I saw Him through prayer and worship. He showed himself to me through His Word. However, I didn't learn the Bible just by studying it alone, I learned also by what I went through. I prayed and quoted scriptures to keep myself sane so I could get healing, keep my heart right, my thoughts clear, and learn how to love others even when they may be against me. I wouldn't change anything I went through other than I wish I had known and trusted God sooner.

When I was broke and in a very bad place, God provided for me and my family. When I was diagnosed with lupus and doctors said I would be crippled, God wouldn't let me look up anything about the disease. I refused to agree with what I was feeling, believing God would heal me. Whenever you are overwhelmed, worship and declare the Word. He can bring forth healing.

When one of my clients of 14 years was about to pass away, I could feel it. I asked God not to let her die on my shift because she was not only my client but my friend. I would help her even when I wasn't on the schedule. The morning of her death, she was doing good when I was leaving. She had an appointment at nine. I left her home at seven. We joked about her appointment and about her trying to sneak to Kmart on the way home. Shortly after nine a.m., I received a call telling me she had passed away (God answered my prayer).

I remember not paying a gas bill for over 7 years. I called often to make sure the credit given was correct. God is too good to me to steal or to do anything out of His will. He kept me from accidents and helped my children with things they were going through.

There was a time I drove to church on bald tires. God had someone to purchase me a full set of brand-new tires. We love because He first loved us.

I remember when I first felt God wrap His arms around me. I was crying because I felt like I had let Him down after all He had done for me. I was in a place of repentance and sorrow when I felt two arms hug me. It is a feeling and experience I will always remember. I knew then God really loved me…for real. He shows me more and more His love for me. But the main reason I love and need Him is because He first loved me. 1 John 4:19 NIV: "We love Him because He first loved us." Now that I understand this it makes it easier to love others as well.

I love Him because He is the keeper of my soul. He has given me grace and mercy over and over. I love Him because

John 3:16 NIV says, "For God so loved the world, that he gave his only begotten son, that whosoever believes in him should not perish, but have eternal life."

He made so many ways for me when I did not see a way. I love Him because He looked beyond my faults and saw my needs. I love Him because He sent His son to die on the cross for me. I am 100 percent team Jesus, but I can only give you my experience with Him. I hope you will make your decision to receive Him and to hold on to Him if you already know Him.

God loves you with an everlasting love. He has promises waiting on you. I pray for you to find the love He wants to show you and give you. He is an amazing God and Lord.

God has been so very good to me. He has shown me His love is real. I am grateful and blessed because He loves me. There is no greater love shown in this earth. This is why I need Him.

Let us pray:

Father, for every person that reads this book may they come to love You and have a personal relationship with You, Lord. May they experience Your love on a new level and share it with others.

Father, love away our hurt and pain. Wipe away our tears. Heal our brokenness. Love away the anger. Deliver us from everything that is not like you. Bring us to the truth of Your Word and help us to love You and others, for the enemy has brought division, false teachings, and misunderstanding to get our focus off of You. But, Father, You said perfect love casts out fear.

Father, we need your love in all areas of our lives. Heal us and make us whole. We want to have life and to have it more abundantly. We need You if we are to find peace and have strength. We need your grace and mercy daily.

Father, we pray that your love will never fail; that it will keep us drawn to You. Let Your love shine through us that people will see You through us and in us. In Jesus' name. Amen.

Take a moment to tell God you love Him. Ask Him to shower His love on you. Write down an experience you had with God that was a reminder of His love.

Why Do I Need Him?

- I need Him to be Lord of my life.
- I need Him to give me peace.
- I need Him to bring healing.
- I need Him to keep my children and family safe.
- I need Him to renew my strength when I am weak.
- I need Him to give me wisdom.
- I need Him so I can love my neighbor as I love myself.
- I need Him because of the grace and mercy He gives daily.
- I need Him because he is my everything.
- I need Him because I am nothing without Him.

Acts 17:28 NIV says: "For in him we live and move and have our being: even some of your own poets have said we are his offspring."

I need Him because I need to be set free from things, many of which I have not talked about in this book, such as a spirit of fear, people pleasing, and a spirit of deception. This book is more about getting free so we can live the life God wants us to live.

Isaiah 61:3 KJV says, "To appoint unto them that mourn in Zion to give them beauty for ashes, the oil of joy for mourning and a garment of praise for the spirit of heaviness, that they might be called trees of righteousness, the planting of the Lord, that he might be glorified."

I will never forget all the things He has done for me. Sometimes, God will bless your enemy to be a blessing to you. I needed him to turn my ashes into beauty. I feel like this is the story of my life. I need Him for my children, family, neighbors, church family, the ministry, our nation, our country, our school system, even for you and so much more. We are commanded to love one another and to have concern for one another. I would not be able to write this book without Him. I give God the glory for all He has done for me.

God has given me wisdom so I can be a blessing to those who have an ear to hear. For our walk He has given us scripture. Each scripture tells *why I need him* and why *you* need him. No one saw the tears I cried when my heart was broken. No one saw the pain I lived through when my body was not allowing me to walk upright. No one saw the agony and turmoil of the loss of my loved ones. No one knew about the molestation, rape, and emotional damage in my life that I kept hidden for quite a long time. No one knew the pain of being a mother and auntie and trying to keep 13 children safe from all the damage I suffered in life. No one knew the feeling of rejection I suffered or how I was hurt not only by the world but by the church.

I thought no one knew but God knew everything. He knew about it all. He turned my ashes into beauty.

Ephesians 3:14-16 NIV, "For this reason I kneel before the Father, from whom every family in heaven and on earth derives its name. I pray that out of his glorious riches he may strengthen you with power through his Spirit in your inner being."

Allowing God to dwell in your heart is one of the richest experiences you will ever have. Knowing Him will bring peace to your life. God said we should be rooted in love.

You must forgive if you want to be forgiven. Yes, it is a process but it is not impossible. God will give you the grace if you truly want to forgive. He wants us to have joy and peace in our lives. Romans 15:13 KJV, "May the God of hope fill you with all joy and peace in believing, so that by the power of the holy spirit you may abound in hope."

Ephesians 4:32 KJV: "And be ye kind one to another, tenderhearted, forgiving one another, even as God for Christ's sake hath forgiven you."

Unforgiveness can stop you from finding true peace. It puts you in a place of not enjoying your life to the fullness. If you want to walk in victory, you need Him to defeat the enemy. 1 Corinthians 15:57 KJV: "But thanks be to God which giveth us the victory through our Lord Jesus Christ."

It has taken a long journey to get to the title of this book, but I wanted it to be last because it brings everything together. Writing this book stirred up emotions; grief came upon me. Closure came to me in some areas, along with understanding and revelation of the Word. I gained more wisdom through my writing. God is awesome.

To the unsaved first—come to know Him. Time is short in the earth. Give your life to Him. Be set free from the cares of this world.

The Word says, "If you confess with your mouth and believe in your heart that God raised Jesus from the dead that you are saved."

John 8:24 Paraphrased, "Unless you believe that I am who I claim to be you will die in your sins."

If you know Him and need to increase your faith or gain a stronger walk, Hebrews 11:1KJV says, "Now faith is the substance of things hoped for, the evidence of things not seen."

2 Corinthians 5:7 NIV: "7 For we live by faith, not by sight."

If you are in between in your decision, see Deuteronomy 30:19 NIV: "I call heaven and earth as witness against you that I have set before your life and death, blessing and cursing, therefore choose life that both thou and thy seed may live."

There are many more reasons and scriptures that allow us to see *we need Him.* I am sold out on Him. It is not because someone *made* me but because He has made himself real in my life. I will trust in Him and lean not to my own understanding as He instructed.

"Trust Him with all your heart and lean not to your own understanding" (Proverbs 3:5-6 paraphrased).

The Word of God is alive and active, sharper than any double-edged sword. It penetrates even to dividing soul and spirit, joint and marrow. It judges thoughts, attitudes, thoughts, and intention of the heart, which are needed to help in your walk.

I hope you will see why you need Him, too. I hope and pray that you will call on Him. He is waiting on you to take responsibility in your walk. Let go of offences, hurt, pain, disappointment, fear, anxiety, and tradition and get into relationship with Him. You have tried everything else in life. You have tried to get it together for so many years. Let go and let God come in and give you victory.

I needed God to come into my life and heal me, make me whole from the brokenness in my life. I needed Him to be my Lord and Savior.

I thank Him for coming into my life and being Lord over me. I thought I did not need anyone, but I had no clue I needed Him. Thank you for allowing me to see truth. Thank you for giving me a chance to repent of my sins. Thank you for healing me and making me whole. I know I have a long way to go but knowing God is with me makes it easier.

I don't know what you need today that you are reading my book, but I do know you can find it in God's loving arms. He loves you. He knows everything you have been through and everything you have done and He doesn't love you any less. He wants you to come to Him so he can take your burdens and give you some rest.

God is the world's greatest super hero. Unlike the fictional super heroes, God is real. They have to change out of their role, God never gets off his throne. As much as I enjoy watching *The Avengers* movie I know who the real world Savior is and always will be.

Let us pray:

Father, thank you for loving us and keeping us throughout our lives. We pray that we become who you called us to be. Use us for your glory and your purpose. We need you clean us up. The world has taught us selfishness. We have been taught that we can make it on our own and that it is ok to look out for you and yours only. This is not what Your Word teaches so help us to come into the knowledge of your truth. Renew in us a right spirit and create in us a clean heart. Increase our faith and bring the Word to life for us. Forgive us for trying to remove You from everything. Without you we are doomed to fail, but through you we are more than conquerors.

Father, thank you that in You we can find deliverance, healing, and salvation. Keep us in our walk. Cover our families and all that concerns us. We will love you with all our heart, mind, and soul. In You we live and have our being. Have your way in our lives. Nevertheless, your will be done.

Father, for those who do not know you, I hope and pray that they will come to know you. For those who are walking with You, Lord, I pray that you come to know the fullness of who God really is and that you walk in the dominion, power, and authority He has given you. All around the world seems to be failing in jobs, health, school system, families and sometimes we are not doing well ourselves. That is why we need You God. In Jesus' name. Amen.

Conclusion

Let go of the past. Renew your thoughts so you can move forward. Before you close this book ask God for the following 7 things.

God, I am asking You to:

1. Renew my mind.
2. Set me free from anything that hinders You.
3. Show me who You are in my life.
4. Allow me to see where You have shown up in my life.
5. Allow me to boldly share my testimony to help others.
6. Help me along my love walk.
7. Show me why I need You.

In closing, it is my prayer that this book has enlightened and triggered something in you to change so you can be free to be who God called you to be. I pray that He allows you to walk in victory. I pray that He brings joy, peace, provision, power, protection and His presence in, over, and through your life.

References

https://en.wikipedia.org/wiki/Loneliness

Other Books by Stacy Rhodes

Free to Be Me
Made Without Excuse

For bulk book purchases, autographed copies, and/or to
arrange speaking engagements with this author:
Contact Stacy Rhodes
stacyneedsjesus@gmail.com

Books available in Print and Digital